THE
COURAGE
TO
HOPE

JAMES MELVIN WASHINGTON

THE
COURAGE
TO
HOPE

FROM BLACK SUFFERING
TO HUMAN REDEMPTION

Edited by

QUINTON HOSFORD DIXIE

and

CORNEL WEST

Foreword by VINCENT HARDING

Essays in honor of James Melvin Washington

Beacon Press

Boston

Beacon Press
25 Beacon Street
Boston, Massachusetts 02108-2892
www.beacon.org

Beacon Press books
are published under the auspices of
the Unitarian Universalist Association of Congregations.

Excerpt from "The Politics of Conversion and the Civilization of Friday"
reprinted from the *Journal of Interdenominational Theological Center*,
vol. XXI, nos. 1 and 2, fall 1993 / spring 1994: 64–80.
Reprinted by permission of JITC.

05 04 03 02 01 00 99   8 7 6 5 4 3 2 1

Text design by Christopher Kuntze
Composition by Wilsted & Taylor Publishing Services

Library of Congress Cataloging-in-Publication Data

The courage to hope : from black suffering to human redemption /
edited by Quinton Hosford Dixie and Cornel West ; foreword by
Vincent Harding.
p.   cm.
Includes bibliographical references.
ISBN 0-8070-0953-9 (pbk.)
1. Afro-Americans—Religion.   I. Dixie, Quinton Hosford.
II. West, Cornel.
BR563.N4C69   1999
277.3′0089′96073—dc21   99-29666

CONTENTS

FOREWORD

The Will to Wrestle: The Courage to Hope

Vincent Harding

I T WOULD BE EASY to be thrown off by the title of this work, confusing its hope with the naïve optimism or facile positive thinking that often passes for hope in our land. The contributors refuse to permit us such a slouching way out. There is nothing easy about hope, and they have found a number of important ways to convey this central message to us. Gathering at the close of the twentieth century, these thoughtful men and women are struggling with issues as ancient and troubling as a black theodicy concerning God's presence amidst the terrors of slavery, and as modern as how to relate to the potential "low-life" morality of the hip-hop generation. With a few crucial exceptions (such as Judith Weisenfeld's own relentless and "secularist" combat with the power of modern evildoers— and Internet corruptors) these witnesses all gather at the river of black Christian faith.

It is with special determination that they confront one particularly challenging topic: the arrival of our own black Christian community in the midst of America's secular, materialist, and often hopeless culture. They seem to be asking, in varied ways: Does anyone at this historical juncture still seek an "authentic Christianity" as our enslaved foreparents once did? Are there any more opportunities for African Americans to offer to humankind some models of hope in the midst of suffering? Or have we determined to abandon our specialization in suffering? Could it be that the households of suffering and the respectable communities of faith have become too deeply separated in our class-riven society?

However, the combat cannot, must not be ignored, for we humans (especially we black Americans) have almost always been most fully transformed in the cauldron of struggle and suffering. Much of the work in this volume calls us to paraphrase James Washington, the gifted preacher, scholar, and teacher whose work serves as the inspiration of this collection. The collection also evokes the message of another Washington who called his companions to a long adventure of struggle—Harold Washington, the first black mayor of Chicago. James Washington, the preacher, understood the sermon as "a moment of spiritual combat." On April 29, 1983, Harold Washington proclaimed another "moment of combat": "Most of our problems can be solved. Some of them will take brains, and some of them will take patience, but all of them will have to be wrestled with like an alligator in the swamp."

James Melvin Washington might have called them angels, but he knew, and most of these witnesses know, that there are really alligators as well as angels in the American swamp, in the souls of black folk, in the communities of faith. And the time for wrestling is upon us—again.

INTRODUCTION

The Intellectual Legacy of James Melvin Washington

Quinton Hosford Dixie

Nonetheless, as a black Christian permitted to rise out of the
depths of Afro-America's working class, and now as a scholar,
teacher, and preacher, I believe I see a glimmer of intellectual
and spiritual hope. That hope emanates from a strange and
faint light. It resides in what may seem like a cynical, obvious,
and even groundless rumor: Afro-Americans are a homeless
people. . . . Despite the fact that this observation is born of despair, I still believe there is hope. Black homelessness has
taught us something about how to cope with modernity which
may be useful to Christians and "pagans" alike. As children of
the Atlantic Slave Trade, we were the first modern people to encounter what the existentialists call "absurdity." And it came
upon us on a massive, continuous scale. . . . Yet even the absurd is experienced in specific contexts and situations. Too
often the bourgeois propensity to spawn sameness and universality erroneously homogenizes human experience. Diversity
is located in the nuances of human experience.

—JAMES MELVIN WASHINGTON

JAMES MELVIN WASHINGTON was fond of para-
phrasing Jean Paul Sartre's assertion that a man or
woman is defined by his or her project. When James de-
parted the land of the dying on May 7, 1997, he left behind
an extensive body of research and writing that points to his
own understanding of what he deemed to be his project.

As a student of history, Washington employed the tools
of his trade to carve from the past a "stubborn tradition of
loyal opposition in American history."[1] Of course, this
leads one to ask the million-dollar question: who or what

was being so loyally opposed, and by whom? For Washington, this "stubborn tradition" is embodied in, though certainly not limited to, the travails and triumphs of Black Christendom. Indeed, one could safely argue that the story of Black Christendom is one of redemptive suffering. It is the saga of a people's commitment to "embrace the porcupine," so to speak—to engage in a love so tough that the opposition experiences what Kahlil Gibran calls "the pain of too much tenderness." In Washington's formula, the opposition consists of American society in general, and American Christendom in particular. It is an America so arrogant that it equates diversity with the equal opportunity to mirror the dominant culture; and it is a church so self-righteous that it would, at best, see the black religious experience as an "important addendum"[2] to salvation history.

Perhaps the juxtaposition of loyalty and opposition may appear oxymoronic. Yet Washington's scholarly project demonstrates the compatability of the two concepts. His research and writing on Martin Luther King, Jr., the crisis in the sanctity of conscience in American jurisprudence, as well as religion and the Civil Rights Movement confirms a commitment to American ideals, but at the same time, a rejection of the patterns of their selective application.[3] His intellectual legacy illuminates a stubborn tradition of Christians accepting the call to martyrdom in order to "redeem the soul of America." Unfortunately, the nation could rarely look to the Christian churches for any guidance out of the moral minefield of pseudospeciation, for the same racist tendencies that had a choke hold on American society also gripped firmly the country's religious establishment. Despite this moral contradiction, most Af-

rican American Christians defended their faith in the
God of Christianity, while at the same time condemning
the false witness of those who misrepresented the cause
of Christ. From his fastidious workmanship on African
American scholar and theologian John Wesley Edward
Bowen, to his indefatigable interest in black Baptist history
and African American spirituality, Washington illustrates
Black Christendom's quest for an authentic Christianity.[4]

As a historian, James Washington left a legacy of his
own opposition to the historical profession that trained
him. He was acutely aware of the distinction between human history and the historical enterprise. The former is
the entire story of the human race, and the latter represents
those parts of the story historians choose to recall. Hence,
his goal was to call to remembrance the countless narratives of the victims of history, and in the process, to discover "when, where, and how we failed to love them as the
Lord commanded us to do."[5] Washington believed that by
uncovering the hidden stories about the African American
religious experience, perhaps all Americans could learn
something that might prove beneficial to understanding
the experience of nonblacks. Indeed, he contended that
the particularity of human experiences holds important
insights for a broader appreciation of the human condition.

Here, in *The Courage to Hope*, Washington's friends and
colleagues come together to attempt to give a meaning to
black suffering that goes beyond the narrow bounds of racial particularities to unlock the limitless prospects of the
human experience. While the point of inquiry begins with
black suffering, to remain at that point means that one runs
the risk of privileging black pain. The danger in this is that

it places one on a path which leads to the two-headed
dragon of self-pity and self-righteousness. While pain certainly is relative, it is our contention that there are important lessons for all of humanity in the distinctiveness of another's afflictions. Of course, we are not suggesting it is the
only light on the horizon, nor is it the brightest light. Nonetheless, black suffering is a gateway through which humankind may gain access to its own tortured soul. In sum,
it is a "faint light" that leads to human redemption.

Each of the authors in this volume has benefited, however slightly, from James's insatiable research appetite and
his unquenchable thirst for knowledge. Those closest to
James will recall his heartwarming sermon, "The Aristocracy of Faith," in which he outlined a stubborn tradition
of Christians refusing to drop the baton. Now, James
has handed the baton of academic rigor, spiritual insight,
scholarly sensitivity, and intellectual courage to those who
remain to cherish his memory. It is in this same spirit that
we relay some of our own academic and religious pursuits
in honor of one who passed on so much to so many. It is my
hope that this collection of essays lives up to James Melvin
Washington's intellectual legacy.

HISTORY

"God's All in This Place"

*God and Historical Writing in
the Postmodern Era*

David D. Daniels III

GOD CAME UP unexpectedly in an American religious history course I taught in the 1980s at a seminary in mid-town Manhattan. My class was examining the causes of the eruption of a religious movement near the end of the colonial era in American history. After compiling a seemingly exhaustive list, ranging from economic to political to psychological, one student asked me why God was omitted. Initially, I was taken aback. God failed to make both my list of causes gleaned from the secondary literature and the one presented by my professors in my doctoral history program. But the seminarian did not merely seek to add God to the list; he wondered why God was not being considered the essential cause of the movement.

My response was feeble but firm, stressing that identifying God as a cause is a theological decision, not a historical judgment. History, I reflected, studies topics open to scrutiny and analysis, and God is closed to historical analysis. I argued that modern historical scholarship has modeled itself after the scientific quest for observation and verification, and that historians consider the appeal to God as the cause of a phenomenon as a sign of intellectual sloth. God, for them, is the easy way out of the arduous intellectual labor needed to ascertain causes that are not simplistic.

While I concluded the conversation in my history class by relegating Godtalk to theology courses, the question stayed in my mind: can God be a subject in historical inquiry? Karen Armstrong recently entitled her book *The History of God*, but Armstrong was interested in God as an idea more than as a subject. The primary documents we read in religious history courses are filled with Godtalk, yet in the historical analyses based on these texts God as a subject is bracketed to allow focus on other causes of religious events.

Is the decision not to explore God as a cause or a context for the growth of a religious movement, for instance, merely an unexamined prejudice that reflects modernity's obsession with science and empiricism and its unequivocal dismissal of God? Should the study of history in the postmodern era confront the possibility of God as a subject? But first, what is it about the postmodern moment that would allow us to entertain God as both a divine agency or presence and a historical subject?

The historical shift from premodernity to modernity to postmodernity is difficult to sketch succinctly, if at all. The first grand shift from premodernity to modernity is often limned as a change from a theocentric world to an anthrocentric world in which economics, politics, and culture were the prime movers in history, and humans as their agents the proper subjects of history. According to the propagandists of modernity, premoderns had employed God to justify superstition, irrationality, ignorance, tyranny, and dogmatism. The flight from enlisting God as the cause forced humanity, in the estimation of moderns, to take responsibility for the world, for the human plight, and to change society for the better. In their scenario a return to God as the subject would be ruinous to human intelligence and the world.

The second grand shift, modernity to postmodernity, is pictured as a transition from an anthrocentric world to either a centerless or a polycentric world characterized by the loss of the subject. According to the purveyors of postmodernity, the moderns used the myths of Reason, the "universal man," and progress to promote universality. The result was that the human world became a unidimensional world, with modern historians employing their master narratives for Eurocentric purposes. History was the arena of Europeans and a few others; Africa was bereft of history. The arena of history—politics and philosophy— was occupied by males; females lived in the ahistorical world of the private sphere. For the emerging postmodern historians of the late-twentieth century, the polycentric shift has produced a turn in which all human lived experience became the subject matter of history. Everyone and everything had a history, even abstractions like tastes, anger, cleanliness, and sexuality. Multiplicity supplanted universality; multidimensionality replaced unidimensionality; multidirectional analyses marginalized progress as a linear approach. Reality, if reality existed, by definition stretched historical categories. Postmodern approaches, then, allow historians to recognize the existence of a vast array of peoples sustaining throughout modernity a distinctly irrational belief in God as a subject.[1]

Conceptually, then, is it possible for God to be interpreted as one of the "subjects" of history within one of the centers in postmodernity's polycentric world? Is such a minimalist move an advancement over modernity's anti-God biases or a disservice to God by limiting God to only one center and defining God as ultimately impotent? The theological issue should not predetermine the historian's response; the historian must ponder the possible without prejudging the theological merits of the historical endeavor. Attention, though, should be given to what such a historiographic move accomplishes.

While postmodern historians might postpone theological reflection, they should overhear the conversations conducted by postmodern philosophers. They discuss God in antifoundationalist and postfoundationalist terms. They resist the temptation to debate the existence of God, yet they refer to God as more than a symbol. Postmodern historians might also eavesdrop on the debates among anthropologists, who have long been exploring the difficulties of probing worldviews or cosmologies drastically different from modernity.

Is the postmodern historian's exploration of God as subject a discussion of divine agency? Would postmoderns construe divine agency differently from premoderns? Modernity introduced the vagaries of human agency. Postmodernity introduced the erasure of the human subject and the vacuousness of the master deterministic schema of Adam Smith, Karl Marx, and Sigmund Freud.

Does the postmodern study of God as "subject" differ when the focus is on divine presence rather than divine agency? Divine presence constrasts the difference between absence and presence in God as subject. Divine absence refers to the spaces and moments where God has seemingly withdrawn or, more deeply, where there is a void in the spaces or moments that God had previously graced. Divine presence serves as a backdrop to the discussion of divine absence, but it also refers to spaces and moments that God has graced. Of course, divine agency necessitates the activity of divine presence/absence. Yet divine presence might refer to the graced places, spaces, and moments where humans encounter God or even "run into God" without God necessarily doing anything to facilitate the encounter, save being present. Divine presence may also refer to the qualitative difference God makes by gracing a place, space, or moment with God's presence. And divine presence may finally refer to how humans negotiate spaces and moments differently because of their recognition of divine presence in a space or moment. How do we conceive of divine presence or absence? Can absence, for instance, be described beyond the traces that God leaves in history? Must the historian, then, initiate a study of the divine traces in history?[2]

An exemplary case is the American Civil Rights Movement, in which a public and provocative display of belief in God's involvement in the struggle emboldened African Americans, both religious and nonreligious, to challenge the legality and the morality of state-sanctioned racial segregation and terrorism. Their claim that "God is on our side" affirmed their belief that they would overcome evil, with God's help. While most civil rights activists who constituted the movement understood and deeply felt that God was pivotal to the campaign to dismantle legalized racial segregation and discrimination, the history texts recounting and reconstructing the Civil Rights Movement erase God as a subject. When God does appear in modern history texts, it is only as the focus of the simplistic faith of a "hyper-religious" African American community.[3]

The Civil Rights Movement to many activists was a reli-

gious moment, a God-filled moment. Andrew Young entitled a chapter in his memoirs, "The Lord Is with This
Movement." Fannie Lou Hamer considered the advent of
the Civil Rights Movement in Mississippi an answer to her
prayers. Martin Luther King, Jr., preached sermons like
Our God Is Able, which accented the capacity of humans to
join with God in defeating evil. Bayard Rustin recounted
on how King combined within himself an "analytical,
philosophical mind" with an amazing sense of an active,
personal God. Ruby Hurley recalled how her activism was
only sustained by "the grace of God." How do we best
interpret this reality without situating it within a cause-
and-effect framework? Can we discuss the reality of the
Civil Rights Movement as an encounter with a God-filled
moment?[4]

Maybe the Civil Rights Movement as a God-filled moment resembled the worship event that constituted the
mass meeting. At this worship event the public and communal expression of the private conversations about local
injustices were aired so that the community could hear
from the residents what the activists had learned. Consequently, the community could be empowered by the telling
of their own stories, the naming and demystifying of their
oppression, and brainstorming about the appropriate collective response to the plight. At these worship events powerless and disfranchised people were transformed into
activists.

The Civil Rights Movement's mass meetings were also
worship events in that they were the products of human
agency, organizational strategies, rhetorical practices, and
liturgical acts on the one hand, yet on the other, they became more than their parts when, like worship, the civil

rights activism erupted into a transformative movement. Possibly the transformative movement echoed a God-filled moment. Private conversations were voiced publicly. Justice and truth defined everyday interactions. In the moments and events that constituted the movement, people cast their activism in terms of responses to God's call to participate; they discovered unknown courage; they exposed the falsity of the seeming normalcy of segregation; they captured the popular imagination and garnered moral capital; they solicited the participation of preexisting institutions to construct the structural base of the movement; and they strategized and dismantled segregation piece by piece. While some of the activists might discuss God in terms of cause and effect, harking back to a premodern image of God, a postmodern historian could explore different frameworks to conceive of these God-filled moments of divine presence and agency.

Historiographically, the challenge would be to continue the trend in civil rights studies of moving beyond King-centered portrayals of the movement as well as other high-profile national and local leaders to focus on institutions and organizational strategies as well as the particularity of local struggles. The task would be to analyze the constitutive elements of the various moments that erupted into the movement, pausing to note traces of God. Merely to substitute God for Martin Luther King, Jr., would be to regress historiography. In the postmodern context, whether the Messiah is King or God is problematic historiographically. The intellectual challenges confronting postmodern thought must be critically engaged.[5]

The historical task of reintroducing God in historical discussions and recognizing God as subject in history is difficult, but not impossible. At this juncture, whether we focus on divine agency, presence, or absence is secondary; the primary assignment is to discover conceptually how to recognize God as subject in history. The historian dedicated to restoring critical conversations about God as a subject in history must take care to preserve the intellectual rigor introduced by the moderns while complicating their accounts with the critique of postmodernity.

PASSAGE AND PRAYER

The Origin of Religion in the Atlantic World

Charles H. Long

PRAYER is at the heart of any religious attitude. It is the open acknowledgment that the individual and the community are dependent upon powers of being outside the human arena. Even before there are words or postures, prayer is an attitude, an orientation, the initial deciphering of a way to be in the world.

Through prayer the gods are evoked and imaged. The religious community is brought into being through prayer and prayer then forms the context of its continued existence. It is difficult to conceive of a religious community that is devoid of prayer; one might say that prayer is the essence of religion, at the very heart of the religious experience. Indeed, prayer reveals both the form and content of the soul.

I. FORMS OF THE SOUL

The phenomenologist of religion, Gerardus van der Leeuw, defines the soul as the locus of the sacred in the human. In his classic, *Religion in Essence and Manifestation*, he sets forth the basic structures of this inner locus of sacrality. He undertakes a phenomenological description of the following orders and structures: The Soul as a Whole; Souls in the Plural; The Form of the Soul; The External

Soul; The Uniquely and Powerful and Divine Soul; The
Immortal Soul; The Creature; The Country of the Soul;
and The Destiny of the Soul.

Underlying all these modalities and comprising the basic "matter" of the soul is what he refers to as "soul-stuff."

> This soul then, as one whole, is connected with some
> specific "stuff." It is not restricted to any single portion
> of the body, but extends itself over all its parts according
> as these show themselves capable of some kind of power-
> fulness, just as the blood is distributed throughout the
> whole body although certain organs are richer in blood
> than others. . . . For the "soul" designates not life and
> nothing more, and still less consciousness, but whatever
> is replete with power and effectiveness. It implies that
> there is a "life" which is more than merely being
> alive. . . .[1]

Van der Leeuw's phenomenological description is exceptional in the manner in which he has shown how the notion
of the soul suggests a material quality of power—what he
refers to as "soul-stuff." This stuff of the soul manifests itself in forms of sacrality and power, thus implying that the
power of being itself, and in this case, the manifestation of
the being of the human, is simultaneously a showing forth
of the sacred and the powerful. His analysis is limited to
the phenomenological realm, and thus the historical dimensions of the manifestation of the soul do not enter into
his study. In addition, the cultural examples are taken from
ancient and so-called primitives cultures.

Let us supplement van der Leeuw's study with another
exemplary statement on the soul in the modern period,
W. E. B. Du Bois's *The Souls of Black Folk*. Du Bois's study
might be seen as a historical phenomenology, specifying
the concreteness of the African American community in

North America; its locus lies in the modern world and its relations and contacts account for the universal intent of its structure. Du Bois in *The Souls* depicts the formation of the trans-Atlantic African soul in its creative and tragic travails of manifestation within the vicissitudes of the modern world. One might observe that Du Bois seems to have taken the last two structures of van der Leeuw's phenomenology of the soul, "The Country of the Soul" and "The Destiny of the Soul," and related them to the order, possibility, and wider dimensions of the African American soul in North America.

II. There Is a River:
Orientation and Beginnings

The most magnificent drama in the last thousand years of human history is the transportation of ten million human beings out of the dark beauty of their mother continent into the new-found Eldorado of the West. *They descended into Hell;* . . . We discern in it no part of our labor movement; no part of our industrial triumph; *no part of our religious experience.*[2]

Since the work of Melville Herskovitts in the 1940s and increasing steadily in subsequent decades, especially in the 1970s, 1980s and 1990s, a number of works have appeared showing the connection and carryover of certain behaviors, artifacts, and other cultural forms from Africa to North America. Fewer works, however, have dealt with the actual passage across the Atlantic itself. Even when works devoted to this dimension have appeared, they have for the most part been devoted to statistical and demographical details of the number of Africans who were enslaved and brought into the world of the Atlantic.

The Middle Passage—chained enslaved Africans in the holds of several ships of every Atlantic maritime nation—was never forgotten by the Africans, neither during slavery nor in freedom. The watery passage of the Atlantic, that fearsome journey, that cataclysm of modernity, has served as a mnemonic structure, evoking a memory that forms the disjunctive and involuntary presence of these Africans in the Atlantic world. From this perspective, religion is not a cultural system, much less rituals or performance, nor a theological language, but an orientation, a basic turning of the soul toward another defining reality.

One hears the refrain in Negro spirituals, such as "Wade in the Water," "Deep River," or "Roll, Jordan, Roll" and in the great Langston Hughes's poem "The Negro Speaks of Rivers." This meaning has also been the inspiration for several scholarly works devoted to African Americans in North America.[3] Obviously, Europeans and Africans were on the same ships in the Atlantic passage, the Europeans seeking a land of opportunity and conquest, the Africans sailing into a land and a life of slavery. They sailed upon the same ship but it is clear that they were making quite different journeys. And the Africans have never forgotten their initiation into the Atlantic world of modernity.

Just as the Mediterranean Sea is the water of the ancient cultures of the world, the Atlantic Ocean is the watery passage of modernity.[4] Fernand Braudel describes three orders of time in the Mediterranean world. The first is the time that expresses the imperceptible rhythms of the environment and the landscapes upon which human beings depend. The second is the time of societies and civilizations—social time. There is finally the time of the individual and the effects of individual acts in human societies. In his discussion of the Mediterranean, Braudel demonstrates how the Mediterranean Sea in its *longue durée* reflects and refracts in a primordial manner the other two notions of time. Braudel has also undertaken a study of the modern world in his three-volume *Civilization and Capitalism.*[5]

Braudel was preceded in this investigation of the making of the Atlantic world by *The Modern World System,* the work of his pupil, Immanuel Wallerstein.[6] Given these and other comprehensive studies of the origins of the Atlantic world of modernity, we find nothing in them of the primordial structures reminiscent of the Mediterranean. On the conventional level, it is clear that the Mediterranean seems to be a womb for the gestation and birth of religions—in van der Leeuw's sense, of soul-stuff—not only the world religions of Judaism, Christianity, and Islam, but the ancient traditions of Zoroaster, of Mani, and the even older traditions of Mesopotamia and Egypt.

The Atlantic world introduces us to the globalization of the meaning of humanity. It creates and intensifies the relationships among and between all peoples on the planet. The Atlantic is, however, not a revealer of deities, seers, and prophets; it is not under the sign of revelation but of freedom, civilization, and rational orders. This world manifests no regard for the layered thickness of time. It is a world justified by the epistemologies of Kant and Descartes, the English empiricists, and the ethical economies of Adam Smith and Marx. The world of the Atlantic lives under the rhetoric and mark of freedom—a freedom that was supposed to banish the specter of the ancient gods and reveal a new and deeper structure to the meaning of human existence. The Atlantic thus reveals no "soul-stuff," no primordial ordering of time or space.

The Atlantic may, nevertheless, be the revealer of a "negative revelation"—a revelation that has insinuated itself within the meanings of all the other relationships of the world of modernity. The Africans secreted within the bowels of slave ships of commerce that bore names like *Brotherhood, John the Baptist, Justice, Integrity, Gift of God, Liberty,* and *Jesus* were equally harbingers of modernity—structures of a primordium of the modern order of the world.[7]

III. WADE IN THE WATERS: THE CONSTITUTION OF THE SOUL

> . . . water symbolizes the whole of potentiality; it is *fons et origo*, the source of all things and of all existence. . . . Principle of what is formless and potential basis of every cosmic principle, container of all seeds, water symbolizes the primal substance from which all forms come and to which they will return either by their own regression or in a cataclysm.[8]

Eliade's descriptive symbolism of water allows us to imagine the potential inherent in a form of the nonhuman world. Water seems to possess its own autonomous structure, which colors and determines the relationship of this form of the world to the human mode of being. Eliade's description, formed as it is within the morphological meaning of religious symbolism, operates in the same nonhistorical mode as Gerardus van der Leeuw's phenomenology.

If we look at this symbolism within the Atlantic world and the Middle Passage, a wider range of symbolic and actual meaning is possible. For the European maritime nations, the Atlantic, with all its ambiguity, is a fascinating reality. From the "discovery" of Columbus to the emergence of the great naval empires of Spain, Holland, England, and France, the Atlantic carried the basic meaning of novelty as *The New World*, a world not only filled with the signs and wonders of the marvelously new, but one that delighted the human spirit in the several modes and opportunities for commercial enterprises; for them it was clear that the Atlantic held forth a surplus of potential. And part of that potential as sign and wonder and commercial enterprise was the tens of millions of Africans who became one of the major cargoes in the establishment of the Atlantic world.

For the Africans in the bowels of the slave ships, the Atlantic represented a cataclysm. As Du Bois put it, "they descended into Hell." Or, as a spiritual remembered it later,

> *And I couldn't hear nobody pray, O Lord,*
> *Couldn't hear nobody pray;*
> *'Way down yonder by myself,*
> *And I couldn't hear nobody pray.*

To whom does one pray from the bowels of a slave ship? To the gods of Africa? to the gods of the masters of the slave vessels? to the gods of an unknown and foreign land of enslavement? To whom does one pray? From the perspective of religious experience, this was the beginning of African American religion and culture. In the forced silence of oppression, in the half-articulate moans of desperation, in the rebellions against enslavement—from this cataclysm another world emerged. This other world was a correlate of, simultaneous with, and parallel to the other Atlantic world. Africans' first expressions of the meaning of the New World took place in the experience of daemonic dread as they were forced into history as terror—the modern world system.

The position set forth here is that African American religion and its subsequent cultures began in the Middle Passage, in that in-betweenness of the continents of Africa, Europe, and the Americas. Africans were brought into the modern world as slave laborers to cultivate sugar, cotton, indigo, rice, and other crops. They worked in factories that manufactured refined sugar, rum, and textiles, served as artisans, fishermen, and boatmen—they were servants of all kinds. They were part and parcel of the entrepreneurial and exploited world that led to mercantilism.

It was not only through slave labor that Africans were insinuated into the modern Atlantic world. Their presence was the occasion around which the problem of value in the New World revolved. The issue may be defined as follows: what is the source of the inherent value of human beings and what or who guarantees the value of the production and exchange of human products? In the Mediterranean world this issue was defined in religious terms that held together the religious and the economic dimensions of human action. The practices and ideologies of the Atlantic world separated these two meanings. Within the modern world of the Atlantic, Africans bodies and their enslaved condition forced the older problematic of religion—the ultimate source of human value.

In a brilliant series of articles appearing in the journal *RES* between 1985 and 1988, William Pietz undertook a comprehensive and critical study of the concept of the "fetish" from its first appearance in Western languages to its present meaning in contemporary scholarly and popular discussions.[9] These articles reveal that one of the major theories concerning the origin of religion was the notion of the "fetish" and fetishism; this origin was identified with Africans and Africa.

More important than this, however, is Pietz's analysis demonstrating how the discourse surrounding the fetish eventuates in a subtle transformation, equal only to the kind of legerdemain in the Cartesian *cogito ergo sum*, that obscures and relocates the issue of both ontological/inherent values on the one hand, and the meaning of value as it relates to production and exchange on the other.

Pietz sets forth four themes in his discussion of the fetish and fetishism:

> 1) the untranscended materiality of the fetish: "matter"
> or the material object, is viewed as the locus of religious
> activity or psychic investment; 2) the radical historicality
> of the fetish origin: arising in a singular event fixing to-
> gether otherwise heterogeneous elements, the identity
> and power of fetish consists of its enduring capacity to re-
> peat this singular process of fixation, along with the re-
> sultant effect; 3) the dependence of the fetish for its mean-
> ing and value on a particular order of social relations,
> which in turn reinforces; and 4) the active relation of the
> fetish object to the living body of an individual: a kind
> of external controlling organ directed by powers outside
> the effected person's will, the fetish represents the a sub-
> version of the ideal of the autonomously determined self.
> ('Fetishism' treats the self as necessarily and in essence
> embodied.)[10]

Pietz in a masterful way demonstrates how fetishism as a theory about the origin of religion in Africa was in one movement applied to the enslaved Africans themselves as a false religion and in another, transferred to the notion of matter and materiality, this time to African bodies, which became a locus of matter in the form of chattel. In the first movement one is able to see how African slaves in North America could be treated as chattel, not persons, and in the other, how all material forms of the world and one's relationship to them could be disenchanted into commodities, unifying the African and the fetish through the language of the commodity. In the larger sense of Atlantic ideologies, slavery might be seen as a fetish of freedom. This mode of thinking and acting became the source of the normalization of alienation as a mark of modernity.

But what of the Africans themselves? Enslaved, deprived of selfhood, separated from their homelands, and lost in a world of strangeness, they had to begin again—from the place and time of a negative utopia. Even before they could make effective the remnants of their former cultures and before they could assimilate elements of the terrifying novelty of their new situation, they had to establish another basis for the human. One might argue that it was the resistance to their enslavement in Africa and aboard the slave ships, or, on the other hand, the simple desire to survive, in spite of the odds. In a more complex manner we might also surmise that their very being expressed the influx of what van der Leeuw has called "soul-stuff" into the Atlantic world and into the world of modernity: *life is more than being alive.* From this primordium of soul-stuff another order of modernity has grown from the complex ambiguity of the Atlantic world.

It expresses itself in resistance, prayer, and the ability to survive. It opens the community to the appreciation of the inviolable dignity of other persons and provides for an alternate meaning of the human as a free person. In speaking about freedom in the modern world, David Brion Davis had this to say: "man's true emancipation, whether physical or spiritual, must always depend on those who have endured and overcome some form of slavery."[11]

"The Blood of the Martyrs Is the Seed of Faith"

Suffering in the Christianity of American Slaves

Albert J. Raboteau

> By some amazing but vastly creative spiritual insight the slave
> undertook the redemption of a religion that the master had
> profaned in his midst. —Howard Thurman

THE DISTINCTIVE character of the religious life of African American slaves, as the black minister, poet, and mystic Howard Thurman attests, consisted in their living witness—despite severe persecution and suffering—to the Christian gospel, whose truth they perceived and maintained in contradiction to the debasement of that very gospel by those who held power over their bodies and their external actions, but not their souls. The suffering witness of slave Christians constitutes a major spiritual legacy not only for their descendants but for the nation as a whole, for any who would take the time to heed the testimony of their words and of their lives.

A Persecuted Faith

If asked to discuss the history of the persecution of Christianity, most of us would first recall the early centuries of the Church as *the* era of persecution, when thousands of Christians became confessors or martyrs by suffering or dying for their faith at the hands of the Roman authorities, until the Emperor Constantine gave official state approval to Christianity in the fourth century. And we probably would mention the modern waves of persecution that swept over Christians in the twentieth century under the antireligious regimes of Communist states in Eastern Europe. Few, I think, would identify the suffering of African American slave Christians in similar terms as a prime example of the persecution of Christianity within our own nation's history. And yet the extent to which the Christianity of American slaves was hindered, proscribed, and persecuted justifies applying the title "confessor" and "martyr" to those slaves who, like their ancient Christian predecessors, bore witness to the Christian gospel despite the threat of punishment and even death at the hands, not of "pagans," but of fellow Christians.

The Christianity of American slaves was born in suffering, the suffering of capture, Middle Passage, and enslavement for life—all justified by Christian European and American defenders of slavery as a means of bringing pagan Africans to the knowledge of Christianity. For despite the physical suffering of slavery, Africans, according to this argument, would gain the spiritual benefits of Christianity and European civilization. The hypocrisy of this argument became clear when slaveholders in the Americas proved apathetic if not downright hostile to the religious instruction of their slaves. It was the labor of Africans' bodies, not the salvation of their souls, that preoccupied the majority of slaveholders, especially in British North America, where whites feared that baptism would disrupt their system of slave control. Peter Kalm, a Swedish traveler in America from 1748 to 1750, outlined their antipathy to Christian slaves:

> It is . . . greatly to be pitied, that the masters of these ne-
> groes in most of the English colonies take little care of
> their spiritual welfare, and let them live on in their Pagan
> darkness. There are even some, who would be very ill
> pleased at, and would by all means hinder their negroes
> from being instructed in the doctrines of Christianity; to
> this they are partly led by the conceit of its being shame-
> ful, to have a spiritual brother or sister among so despica-
> ble a people; partly by thinking that they should not be
> able to keep their negroes so meanly afterwards; and
> partly through fear of the negroes growing too proud,
> on seeing themselves upon a level with their masters in
> religious masters.[1]

It is clear that Anglo-Americans feared the precise ethos that the slaves quickly recognized and valued in Christianity: the incorporation of Africans into the church community changed the relationship of master and slave into one of brother and sister in Christ, a relationship that inevitably contradicted the racist belief in black inferiority upon which slavery depended.

At first the masters reasoned that it would be illegal to hold a fellow Christian in bondage, so baptizing slaves would in effect free them. Colonial legislatures quickly passed laws stating that baptism had no such effect. Nonetheless, slaveowners still resisted missions to convert the slaves. To baptize Africans seemed inappropriate since it made them more like the English, thus blurring the religious difference between blacks and whites, which along with nationality, skin color, and language, formed the ethnic identity of Anglo-Americans and their sense of racial superiority. Moreover, they believed that Christianity would inflate the slaves' sense of self worth and so encourage them to insolent or even rebellious behavior. Christianity, according to this view, ruined slaves. Colonial missionaries argued, to the contrary, that religious instruction would make slaves better slaves by stressing that Christianity made no alteration in social conditions but taught each person to remain content in his station in life. Christianity would induce the slaves to obey their masters out of a sense of duty to God rather than merely out of fear of man. They appealed repeatedly to Ephesians 6:5: "Slaves be obedient to your masters." Thus Christian missionaries came to propagate the gospel as a means of slave control.

Slaves eventually did hear the message of the gospel and insisted, contrary to missionaries and masters, that becoming Christian should result in their (or at least their children's) freedom. Time and again European-American clergymen complained that slaves were seeking baptism because they thought the sacrament would make them free. What the slaves affirmed and the slaveholders rejected was the belief that slavery and Christianity were incompatible—that a slaveholding Christianity was a contradiction in terms, in other words, a heresy. In one of the earliest documents we have from American slaves, they boldly confessed their belief that slavery violated the fundamental law of Christian community, the law of love:

> There is a great number of us sencear . . . members of the Church Christ . . . Bear ye onenothers Bordens How can the master be said to Beare my Borden when he Beares me down with the Have chanes of slavery and operson against my will . . . how can the slave perform the duties of a husband to a wife or parent to his child[?][2]

Slaveowners were well aware that slaves interpreted Christianity as sanctioning their desire for freedom in this life as well as the next. The slaves, therefore, if they wanted to express their faith openly, had to steal away to clandestine prayer meetings in their cabins, woods, thickets, hollows, and brush arbors, the aptly named "hush harbors," nineteenth-century equivalents of the ancient catacombs. There, out from under the eye of the master, they challenged the heresy of the master's preachers with the orthodox doctrine of their own preaching. Lucretia Alexander, a former slave, contrasted the white preacher's version of the gospel with that of her father:

> The preacher came and . . . He'd just say, "Serve your masters. Don't steal your master's turkey. Don't steal your master's chickens. Don't steal your master's hawgs. Don't steal your master's meat. Do whatsomever your master tells you to do." Same old thing all the time. My father would have church in dwelling houses and they had to whisper. . . . Sometimes they would have church at his house. That would be when they would want a real meetin' with some real preachin'. . . . They used to sing their songs in a whisper and pray in a whisper.[3]

As Henry Atkinson, an escaped slave from Virginia, put it, "The white clergymen don't preach the whole gospel there."[4] The hunger for "Real preachin'," that is, the authentic gospel, drove the slaves to gather for their own worship services.

Slave Christians suffered severe punishment if they were caught attending secret prayer meetings, which whites proscribed as a threat to social order. Moses Grandy reported that his brother-in-law Isaac, a slave preacher, "was flogged, and his back pickled" for preaching at a clandestine service in the woods. His listeners were also flogged and "forced to tell who else was there." Grandy claimed that slaves were often flogged "if they are found singing or praying at home." Gus Clark reported: "My Boss didn' 'low us to go to church, er to pray er sing. Iffen he ketched us prayin 'er singin' he whupped us." According to another ex-slave, "the white folks would come in when the colored people would have prayer meeting, and whip every one of them. Most of them thought that when colored people were praying it was against them. For they would catch them praying for God to lift things out of their way." Henry Bibb's master threatened him with five hundred lashes for attending a prayer meeting conducted by slaves on a neighboring plantation without permission. The master who threatened Bibb was a deacon in the local Baptist Church.[5]

In 1792, Andrew Bryan and his brother Sampson were arrested and hauled before the city magistrates of Savannah, Georgia, for holding worship services. Together with about fifty of their followers, they were imprisoned twice and were severely whipped. Andrew told his persecutors "that he rejoiced not only to be whipped, but *would freely suffer death for the cause of Jesus Christ*."[6] When the master's will conflicted with God's, slaves faced a choice: to obey God or to obey man. Some, empowered by the belief that salvation lay in obeying God rather than man, chose to disobey their masters. Eli Johnson, for example, claimed that when he was threatened with five hundred lashes for holding prayer meetings, he stood up to his master and declared, "In the name of god why is it, that I can't after working hard all the week, have a meeting on Saturday evening? I'll suffer the flesh to be dragged off my bones . . . for the sake of my blessed Redeemer."[7] James Smith, a fugitive slave, had been a preacher in Virginia. To prevent him from preaching, his master kept him tied up all day on Sundays and, when he refused to stop, flogged him as well. Nevertheless, Smith kept up his ministry and later reported that "many were led to embrace the Savior under his preaching."[8]

The husband of Candace Richardson, from Mississippi, stole off to the woods to pray, "but he prayed so loud that anybody close around could hear," and so was discovered and punished. Many years later, Mrs. Richardson told interviewers that "beatings didn't stop my husband from praying. He just kept on praying and it was his prayers, and [those of] a whole lot of other slaves that cause you young folks to be free today."[9] A former slave revealed the source of their resolve: "When I was a slave my master would sometimes whip me *awful*, specially when he knew I was praying. He was determined to whip the Spirit out of me, but he could never do it, for de more he whip the more the Spirit make me *content* to be whipt.[10]

Finally, Charlotte Martin, a former slave from Florida, told an interviewer that "her oldest brother was whipped to death for taking part in one of the religious ceremonies."[11] Unfortunately we don't know his name, but Charlotte Martin's brother, and other slaves—unnamed and unknown—joined the company of all those Christians over the ages who have suffered brutal violence and even death to worship God in spirit and in truth. These secret liturgies constituted the heart and source of slave spiritual life, the sacred time when they brought their sufferings to God and experienced the amazing transformation of their sadness into joy.

A SAD JOYFULNESS

Recalling the character of their secret religious gatherings, one former slave declared, "Meetings back there meant more than they do now. Then everybody's heart was in tune, and when they called on God they made heaven ring. It was more than just Sunday meeting and then no godliness for a week. They would steal off to the fields and in the thickets and there . . . they called on God out of heavy hearts."[12] Exhausted from a day of work that stretched from dawn ("day clean") to after sundown, the slaves found relief and refreshment in prayer, as Richard Caruthers remembered: "Us niggers used to have a prayin' ground down in the hollow and sometime we come out of the field . . . scorchin' and burnin' up with nothin' to eat, and we wants to ask the good Lawd to have mercy. . . . We takes a pine torch . . . and goes down in the hollow to pray. Some gits so joyous they starts to holler loud and we has to stop up they mouth. I see niggers git so full of the Lawd and so happy they draps unconscious."[13] This paradoxical combination of suffering and joy permeated slave religion, as the slave spirituals attest:

> *Nobody knows de trouble I see*
> *Nobody knows but Jesus,*
> *Nobody knows de trouble I've had*
> *Glory hallelu!*[14]

The tone of joyful sadness that echoed and reechoed in the slaves' religious worship was eloquently explained by a former slave who was initially puzzled by it himself:

The old meeting house caught on fire. The spirit was there Every heart was beating in unison as we turned our minds to God to tell him of our sorrows here below. God saw our need and came to us. I used to wonder what made people shout, but now I don't. There is a joy on the inside, and it wells up so strong that we can't keep still. It is fire in the bones. Any time that fire touches a man, he will jump.[15]

Joyful sorrow, sorrowful joy, or more accurately, sorrow merging into joy arose from the suffering of the slaves'

lives, a suffering that was touched, however, and so transformed, by the living presence of God.

We all know something of the brutality that slaves endured; and it still is painful to think of it. Yet the mystery
of their suffering took on meaning in the light of the suffering of Jesus, who became present to them in their suffering
as the model and author of their faith. As one former slave
explained to a missionary during the Civil War:

> I could not hab libbed had not been for de Lord . . .
> neber! Work so late, and so early; work so hard, when
> side ache so. Chil'en sold; old man gone. All visitors,
> and company in big house; all cooking and washing all
> on me, and neber done enough. Missus neber satisfied—
> no hope. Noting, noting but Jesus, I look up. O Lord!
> how long? Give me patience! patience! O Lord! Only
> Jesus know how bad I feel; darsn't tell any body, else get
> flogged. Darsn't call upon de Lord; darsn't tell when sick.
> But . . . I said Jesus, if it your will, I will bear it.[16]

The passion of Jesus, the suffering servant, spoke deeply
to the slaves, the sorrow and pain of their life resonating
with his. For if Jesus came as the suffering servant, the
slave certainly resembled him more than the master. They
knew that their lives fit the gospel pattern: "Blessed are the
poor, for theirs is the kingdom of heaven. Blessed are the
meek, for they shall inherit the earth. Blessed are those
who hunger and thirst after righteousness, for they shall be
filled."

The slaves perceived in their own experience the paradox of the gospel, the redemptive power of Christ's suffering, repeated once again in the pattern of their own lives.
They believed that according to this gospel the victory of
evil over good is only apparent. They believed that for
those who follow his way of the cross, sadness yields to joy,
despair to hope, and death to life. This was no easy faith

for slaves exposed to constant toil and regular violence at the hands of professed fellow Christians. We should not underestimate the difficulty of living such beliefs. The temptations to despair, to reject Christianity as a religion for whites, to abandon belief in a God who permits the innocent to suffer were very real. Frederick Douglass, for example, spoke of "the doubts arising . . . partly from the sham religion which everywhere prevailed" under slavery, doubts which "awakened in my mind a distrust of all religion and the conviction that prayers were unavailing and delusive."[17] A free black woman named Nellie, from Savannah, Georgia, confessed "it has been a terrible mystery, to know why the good Lord should so long afflict my people, and keep them in bondage,—to be abused, and trampled down, without any rights of their own,—with no ray of light in the future. Some of my folks said there wasn't any God, for if there was he wouldn't let white folks do as they have done for so many years."[18] One of the sources that sustained Christian slaves against such temptations to despair was the Bible with its accounts of the mighty deeds of a God who miraculously intervenes in human history to cast down the mighty and to lift up the lowly, a God who saves the oppressed and punishes the oppressor. The biblical stories became their story. Why trust that God would deliver them? Because he had, as the spirituals recounted, fit Joshua for the battle of Jericho, rescued Daniel from the lion's den, saved the three Hebrew children from the fiery furnace, kept doubting Peter from sinking beneath the waves, comforted weeping Mary in the garden, and freed Paul and Silas from jail. "Didn't my Lord deliver Daniel? Why not every man?" One biblical story in particular fired the imagination of the slaves and anchored their hope of deliverance.

Exodus

Questioned by her mistress about her faith, a slave woman named Polly explained why she resisted despair: "we poor creatures have need to believe in God, for if God Almighty will not be good to us some day, why were we born? When I heard of his delivering his people from bondage I know it means the poor African."[19] The story of Exodus inculcated in the slaves (and in their descendants) a sense of being a specially chosen people, whose election and destiny were of historic importance in the providence of God. For black Americans the Exodus story took on the force of a prophecy that directly contradicted the dominant image of America as the Promised Land. From the earliest period of their migration to America, British colonists had spoken of their journey across the Atlantic as the exodus of a New Israel from bondage in Egypt to the Promised Land of milk and honey. For African Americans the journey was reversed: whites might claim that America was a new Israel, but blacks knew that it was Egypt, since they, like the children of Israel of old, still toiled in bondage. Unless America freed God's African children, this nation would suffer the plagues that had afflicted Egypt.

Exodus proved that slavery contradicted God's will and so would inevitably end. The where and the how remained hidden in divine providence, but the promise of deliverance was certain. The racist belief that black people were destined by providence and by nature to be nothing more than drawers of water and hewers of wood was false. They were elect of God.

The slaves' sense of identification with the children of Israel was driven deep into their self-awareness by the song, sermon, prayer, and dance of worship. They dramatically reenacted the travails and triumphs of God's chosen people and so affirmed and reaffirmed—contrary to racist doctrines of black inferiority—their own value as a special, divinely chosen people. In their prayer services, biblical past became present in sacred, liturgical time and the stories they sang about came alive. Once again God sent Moses to tell "ol' Pharaoh to let my people go." Once again the mighty wind of God parted the Red Sea so the Hebrew children could cross over dry shod. Once again Pharaoh's army "got drownded."

Long after slavery, African Americans continued to appropriate the story of Exodus to symbolize their common history and common destiny, as a specially chosen, divinely favored people, another, darker Israel denying the dominant myth of America's identity and purpose. In the midst of dehumanizing conditions so bleak that despair seemed the only appropriate response, African Americans believed that God would "make a way out of no way." Enslaved, they predicted that God would free them from bondage. Impoverished, they asserted that "God would provide." Their belief in God did not consist so much in a set of propositions as in a relationship of personal trust that God was with them. As a slave spiritual attests:

> He have been wid us, Jesus,
> He still wid us, Jesus,
> He will be wid us, Jesus
> Be wid us to the end.

As some critics of black religion have long observed, an overemphasis upon religious trust can foster in oppressed people a passive and compensatory otherworldliness vulnerable to fatalism and lethargy. But religious faith also encouraged confidence among African Americans that change was possible in this world, not just in the next, and so enabled black people to hope, and when possible, to act. When acts of external resistance proved impossible, or suicidal, African American spirituality supported internal resistance that was symbolic but nonetheless real. The most effective ground for resisting the demons of dehumanization and internalized racism was the slaves' firm conviction that the human person is made in the image of God.

THE ALTAR OF THE HEART

Drawing upon the worship traditions of Africa, as well as those of evangelical Christianity, African American slaves formed a ritual equivalent to the spirit-empowered ceremonies of their African forebears. Both traditions assumed that authentic worship required an observable experience of the divine presence. "It ain't enough to talk about God, you've got to feel him moving on the altar of your heart," as one former slave explained.[20] Ritual, in this perspective, was supposed to bring the divine tangibly into this world, so that humans might be transformed, healed, and made whole. The presence of God became manifest in the words, the gestures, and the bodies of the believers. In this form of African American worship the divine was embodied in the faithful. The emotional ecstasy of the slaves' worship expressed their profound belief that the preeminent place of God's presence in this world is the person. His altar is the human heart. Moreover, it is the whole person, body as well as spirit, that makes God present. In religious worship—dance, prayer, sermon, and song—the human person, embodied spirit and inspirited body, became an icon of God. A radically personal vision of life flowed from this kind of liturgy. Christian slaves fought off slavery's terrible power to depersonalize its victims by experiencing themselves as images of the divine. Anything, then, that defaced this human image of God was sacrilegious.

In addition to the communal experience of worship, the individual slave's experience of conversion effectively reaffirmed the dignity and worth of the slaves as children of God. Events of great spiritual power, conversions involved a deep reorienting of the values and direction of the convert. The life of the individual slave became part of the age-old struggle between good and evil, a drama of cosmic importance. Slaves spoke of conversion as an experience of rebirth, of being made entirely new, of being filled with love for everything and everybody. To experience, as they did, the unconditional love of God shattered the mentality of slavery. They realized—and realized with the heart, not just the head—that they were of infinite worth as children of God. The conversion experience grounded their significance in the unimpeachable authority of almighty God, no matter what white people thought and taught. They knew that they constituted a spiritual aristocracy, family members in the long genealogy of prophets, apostles, saints, and martyrs made up of those who did not simply talk about God, but experienced His power upon the altars of their hearts. "We be holy; you not be holy," as a group of slaves remarked to their mistress after their conversion. We might expect that their identification with the biblical children of Israel, with Jesus, the suffering servant, and with the saints and martyrs of Christian tradition might have pushed the slaves toward self-righteousness and racial chauvinism. Instead, it inspired compassion for all who suffer, even occasionally for their white oppressors. William Grimes, for example, a slave who refused to lie or to steal, was unjustly accused and punished by his master. "I forgave my master in my own heart for all this, and prayed to God to forgive him and turn his heart," Grimes reported.[21] Mary Younger, a fugitive slave who escaped to Canada, remarked: "if those slaveholders were to come here, I would treat them well, just to shame them by showing that I had humanity."[22] When slaves forgave and prayed for slaveholders, they not only proved their humanity, they also displayed to a heroic degree their obedience to Christ's command: "Love your enemies. Do good to those who persecute and spitefully use you."

COMPASSION

Out of the religion of American slaves a music arose that constituted one of this nation's most significant contributions to world culture. This music spread the message of the slaves' religious legacy far and wide. People around the world have been moved by the capacity of slave spirituals to take the particular suffering of black people in America and extend it into a parable of universal human experience. Gandhi spoke for many when he remarked to Howard and Sue Bailey Thurman that the spirituals got to "the root of the experience of the entire human race under the spread of the healing wings of suffering."[23] What meaning can we glean from the slaves' suffering?

There is no virtue in suffering for its own sake. To romanticize suffering, poverty, and oppression—as affluent American sometimes do—trivializes injustice and leaves unchanged the conditions that cause suffering. Conversely, to shun suffering at all costs is futile. Suffering is an inescapable part of the human condition for masters as well as slaves, for the rich no less than the poor. On this human existential level, the slave experience teaches us that suffering must be lived through; it can't be avoided by any of the spurious means of escape that people use to distract one another from real life. Life is bittersweet, joyful sadness. Unless we realize and accept our radical contingency, our mortality, we succumb to illusion, the illusion that we are omnipotent, that we are in control of our lives. We feed this illusion by preoccupying ourselves with an ever-spiraling cycle of needs, pretending that we have no needs that we cannot ourselves meet, in a vain attempt to deny our suffering and death. These illusions of power become dangerous when we try—as did the slave holders—to live them out by exercising power over others. This deformation of our humanity takes on exceptional force because it is driven by a deep, usually unconscious, fear. The vicious cycle of need-gratification-need that drives modern consumer culture distracts us from facing our fear of suffering and death. The spirituals, as Gandhi and others appreciated, speak of an alternative. They reveal the capacity of the human spirit to transcend bitter sorrow and to resist the persistent attempts of evil to strike it down.

Moreover, Christianity taught the slaves that God had entered into the world and taken on its suffering, not just the regular suffering of all creatures that grow old and die, but the suffering of the innocent persecuted by the unjust, the suffering of abandonment and seeming failure, the suffering of love offered and refused, the suffering of evil apparently triumphant over good. They learned that God's compassion was so great that He entered the world to share its brokenness in order to heal and transform it. The passion, death, and resurrection of Jesus began and effected the process of that transformation. It was compassion, the love of all to the extent of sharing in their suffering, that would continue and bring to completion the work of Christ. All of this of course was paradoxical. All of this of course was a matter of faith.

American slaves accepted that faith. And in doing so they found their lives transformed. No, the suffering didn't stop. Many died still in bondage. And yet they lived and died with their humanity intact, that is, they lived lives of inner freedom, lives of wisdom and compassion. For their condition, evil as it was, did not ultimately contain or define them. They transcended slavery because they believed God made them in His image with a dignity and value that no slaveholder could efface. When white Christians desecrated the gospel by claiming that it supported racial slavery, they defended true Christianity against this false heresy, even at the risk of their lives.

Reflecting theologically upon their experience of suffering as a people, African Americans came to believe that those who oppress and enslave others, those who spread "civilization and the gospel" by conquest, those who degrade other races, those who turn Christianity into a clan religion have already been condemned. Whereas, those who were oppressed but did not oppress, those who were enslaved but did not enslave, those who were hated but did not hate have already entered the kingdom of the one who judges us all according to the measure of our compassion. "As long as you did it to the least of these, you did it to me."

Toward the end of her life, a ninety-year-old former

slave, Maria Jenkins, replied to an interviewer who asked her if all her people were dead: "De whole nation dead," she said, "De whole nation dead—Peggy dead—Toby dead—all leaning on de Lord." And yet, the dead are not gone. Peggy, Toby, Charlotte Martin and her brother, Candace Richardson, Lucretia Alexander, Henry Bibb, Andrew and Sampson Bryan, Richard Caruthers and many, many more are here with us. They live on—a veritable cloud of witnesses.

PROVIDENCE AND THE
BLACK CHRISTIAN CONSENSUS

*A Historical Essay on the African American
Religious Experience*

Sandy Dwayne Martin

PROVIDENCE has played a vital role in the African American religious experience. Indeed, it is part of what I regard as the Black Christian Consensus—the mainstream elements of thought and practice regarding religion among African Americans and its relationship with secular activities in the United States. Specifically, providence within the Black Christian Consensus holds that black people and their spiritual and political struggles operate under the providential care of God and that they have a special mission to demonstrate true Christianity and perfect the American system of democracy. Thus, the Black Christian Consensus constitutes the religious and political consensus among African Americans. As the term indicates, that consensus has been distinctly Christian—and, more precisely, evangelical Protestant. Furthermore, it has extolled, not rejected, the ideals of American democracy, though painfully aware that for blacks those ideals have not materialized. But to understand the historical march of African Americans, religiously and otherwise, as well as any attempt to fashion an ideology or theology of liberation, we must be cognizant of that Consensus. This essay examines this Black Christian consensus as it specifically applied to the concept of providence in the American experience, examining its origins and endurance, and the severe challenges to it during the twentieth century.

THE FORMATION OF THE
BLACK CHRISTIAN CONSENSUS

First, we should comprehend the importance of providence for general Christianity, since that is the overwhelming majority tradition of African Americans. Besides being a synonym for the personal God (in a theistic system), providence is an expression of God's purpose, denotes the Almighty's sovereignty, wisdom, control, and concern for the world, and interprets people's place in God's universe. Providence says that God is in control of the universe and people of God play instrumental roles in God's effecting the divine will among humanity. Scholars such as Albert J. Raboteau have noted that both white and black Christian Americans embraced the concept of providence, applying it to their particular sociocultural circumstances. White settlers in colonial America saw themselves as the chosen people of God subduing the wilderness and setting up a righteous order. Black Christians, on the other hand, were the chosen people expecting God's deliverance from bondage, freeing them to share with the world insights into religion and democracy gained from the crucible of oppression.[1] The journey of blacks from Africans to African Americans during the colonial era entailed the rejection, however slowly, of traditional African ways and the embrace of Christianity.[2] Circumstances in North America cried out for an altered view of providence. Continental Africans of traditional religions understood the providence of the generally remote Supreme Being mediated through the various deities of the individual ethnic groups. Africans in colonial North America required that this one Supreme Being become much more immediate and that the lesser deities recede. In the colonies, African peoples were becoming a true "melting pot," their various ethnicities and religious perspectives being molded into one people. It was in the colonies, not on the Mother continent, that the Yoruba, Ibo, Ashanti, and Fante would become true Africans, transcending their particular ethnic identities and discovering a collective self-identity as one race of people, something discovered much earlier by Europeans. This new collective racial consciousness of being first and foremost African required one Supreme Being who had a plan and a purpose that included this one group of people. That need was met in Christianity.

There is the folk or popular tendency in black America to follow the erroneous examples of individuals such as Malcolm X and associate Christianity with slavery and Islam with freedom. Islam had a comparably long history in western portions of Africa, from whence many Africans were sold, a strong belief in divine providence, a significant presence among Africans brought to the Western hemisphere, and it was not the religion of the white slaveholders.[3] Given these factors, why did Africans in the colonies prefer Christianity to Islam?

I would suggest a number of reasons for the ascendancy of Christianity. First, Islam was never the dominant religion among Africans in North America. Estimates on the percentage of Muslims among the transported African slaves range from six percent to a generous twenty-five per-

cent. Thus, Muslims, according to the most generous estimates, never accounted for more than a fourth of African
slaves. Second, contrary to much popular (and even some
scholarly) opinion there was no easy equation, in the
minds of whites or blacks, of Islam with freedom and
Christianity with slavery. Rather, evidence suggests that,
attempts to utilize Christianity as a tool to promote slavery notwithstanding, white slaveholders generally looked
askance at efforts to Christianize enslaved blacks for a pan-
oply of economic, cultural, psychological, political, and
religious reasons. Conversely, evidence suggests that noted
African Muslims were generally positively connected to the
system of slavery or certainly not viewed as hardened enemies of it. Third, and related to the above point, many African Muslims had been intimately involved in the slave
trade, whereas the African Christian presence was small
and not as connected with the slave trade. Indeed, in North
America prominent Islamic individuals, such as Job Ben
Solomon, Bilali Mohammed, Salih Bilali, Lamine Kebe,
Umar ibn Said, Mohammed Gardo Barquaqua, and Mohammed Ali ben Said, do not appear to have been opposed
to the traffic in slaves or the slave system as such but merely
yearned for freedom and the return to Africa for themselves.[4] Fourth, the conflicts between Muslims and traditional religious peoples on the continent might have sur-
vived in the consciousness of Africans in North America. It
is clear from extant records that Muslims in North America
considered themselves in some sense superior to the "poly-
theists." Fifth, the nature of evangelical Protestantism, its
emphasis on the Bible and its stress on the immediacy of
God's spiritually felt presence, had more direct appeal to
enslaved Africans than Islam. Many biblical stories depict

God rescuing, comforting, and identifying with the deprived and oppressed. Compared to the Christian Bible, the Qur'an, on the other hand, is more a collection of addresses and stories relating to those who are powerful and free. Christianity, and evangelical Protestantism in particular, granted the enslaved a religion that was more mobile and more adaptable to their circumstances. Enslaved Christians did not have to concern themselves with learning still another language (Arabic), ritual prayer five times daily and the attendant rituals of purification connected with it, and pilgrimage to Mecca. Instead, much of the form of traditional African religion—the rhythm, the immediacy of the Divine, improvisation in creating sacred music and prayers—more easily conformed to the experience of evangelical Christianity.

Whatever the main reason or combination of reasons for the enslaved's embrace of Christianity, it is that faith that would provide the context for the black conception of providence and its relationship to African American self-identity. The most successful means of reaching Africans in North America was by means of evangelical Protestant Christianity, as indicated above.[5] The evangelical revivals, the Great Awakening in the first half of the eighteenth century and the Second Awakening in the last decade of the eighteenth and early decades of the nineteenth centuries, provided the opportunity to reformulate and strengthen African (and, increasingly, African American) understanding of the Supreme God and divine providence. Evangelicalism provided similarities of religiosity with African traditional religion and with a much bolder statement of monotheism. The one God of all the earth, including the One who had power over the white oppressors, was with these lowly, oppressed people.

Theodicy, Providence, and
Pan-African Identity

Of course the question of theodicy emerged. If God was the benevolent and all-powerful God of the whole earth, why did Africans suffer estrangement from their continental homeland and brutal chattel slavery, particularly at the hands of many people who also claimed to be Christians? White proponents of evangelizing enslaved blacks and those with antislavery sentiments (the two were often conjoined), as well as black Christians seeking liberation, elaborated what we might term the "Josephite Theology." As the Old Testament Joseph was sold into enslavement by his own brothers, so were the African Josephs betrayed by their African brothers and sisters, who were engaged in an evil traffic for their own selfish reasons. But God used enslavement for a divine purpose, to introduce African Americans to Christianity and Western civilization, regarded as superior to the religion and culture of the Africans. Placed in a providential role like Joseph, the son of Jacob, African Americans would be the means by which these blessings of religion and culture would spread to their continental African kinspeople. Psalms 68:31 ("Princes shall come out of Egypt; Ethiopia shall soon stretch out her hands unto God" in the King James Version) was viewed as a prophecy of the future of the black race. Africa, through the instrumentality of African Americans, would once again rise spiritually and politically, ennobled by the same vibrant faith that had rescued and lifted formerly barbaric white Europe. For slaveholding Christians the message was that they should grant access to missionaries to spread the message on the farms and plantations, and in other places of labor. For those in the antislavery camp, this providential message clearly stated that God did not intend any people to be the slaves of others. In concrete form this theology was expressed in the Puritan classic, *The Selling of Joseph*. It was utilized in attempts to "repatriate" or colonize blacks on the continent, movements supported by the white religious leader Samuel Hopkins in the late eighteenth century and by the American Colonization Society beginning in 1816–17.

Many African Americans would take advantage of this colonization offer, including the Virginia Baptist preacher, Lott Carey, and the African Methodist Episcopal minister and denominational leader, David Coker. During the 1820s, Carey made Liberia his home while Coker journeyed to Sierra Leone, colonies founded by the United States and England, respectively, to provide haven for refugees from slavery and the slave trade. In these cases and in numerous others, these missionary colonizers sought to promote a Christianity that concomitantly propagated their denominations while transcending them. They brought a faith that would contribute to the building of democratic, Christian commonwealths on the African coast, which would in turn evangelize and civilize the rest of Africa. Their grandiose goals were not realized, and such colonizers often found themselves practicing oppression toward the very peoples they sought to save and uplift. But they were deeply convinced that God had called them to these vocations, and such convictions fueled heroic sacrifices and actions.

Other African Americans, including religious leaders such as David Coker's denominational brother, Bishop Richard Allen, deeply distrusted colonization schemes supported by whites, considering them an activity that would depopulate the United States of free blacks and hence solidify the control of the slaveholder. Black leaders understood and even encouraged voluntary efforts on behalf of individuals who sought an Exodus from the land of oppression and journeyed to Promise Lands such as Haiti. The Episcopalian James T. Holly once believed that Haiti would be the land in the Western hemisphere that God would use to develop a strong Christian civilization for the blessing of the black race and the entire world. Later in the century, during the post–Civil War era, other black Christians pursued African missions as a means of working out God's providential plan to Christianize and uplift the black race. As proponents of the earlier African colonization attempts, these black Christians also cited Psalm 68:31 and voiced their belief that of all Christians, African-descended people were most equipped in terms of their physical-climactic suitability and their experience of enslavement to further this providential mission.[6]

PROVIDENCE, INDEPENDENT CHRISTIANITY, AND SLAVERY

Actually, the emergence of racially independent Baptist and Methodist congregations, associations, and denominations during the late eighteenth and early nineteenth centuries reflected this sense of black providential mission. Blacks, especially prior to the Civil War, seceded from white-controlled religious organizations for a number of reasons: to flee racial discrimination, to oppose slavery and other civil constraints more boldly, to worship more freely, to exercise religious leadership unhampered, and to evangelize other blacks whom, they claimed, the white-controlled bodies often overlooked or gave insufficient spiritual attention to. The leaders of these independent bodies made a point of stating that their organizations had an obligation to do for the black race what only members of that race could do successfully. Toward the end of the nineteenth century Bishop James Walker Hood, the AME Zion church historian, made clear his judgment that the movement or exodus of black Christians of an earlier period from white-controlled congregations, associations, and national bodies was part of a larger movement that transcended specific denominations. God had employed the black church to spread a casteless Christianity, oppose enslavement, push for civic freedoms, and give African Americans opportunities to develop leadership, opportunities nowhere more readily available than in the independent African American church, whatever the specific denomination.[7]

James Melvin Washington, in his study of the rise of black Baptist unity during the late 1800s, speaks of this belief in providence among this group of congregational-minded Christians as one involving a black nationalist sentiment that understood God's working through the representatives of a given race to save it. Well into the twentieth century, as many authors have attested, African American Christian leaders saw a providential role for the independent black church as it engaged in the founding of schools, banks, newspapers, and other institutions and instrumentalities for the Christianization and uplifting of blacks both domestically and globally. They included within this providential mission statement the conviction that black Christianity, far better than white Christianity, offered the world an example of the principles of loving God and neighbor.[8]

Antebellum African Americans, both enslaved and free, understood their distinctiveness as children of God and shared a profound sense that God had a providential plan for the black race. We may glean such a theology from the totality of the writings and speeches of abolitionists such as David Walker, Henry H. Garnet, Harriet Tubman, and Frederick Douglass. Douglass made it clear that slaveholding Christians and those who fellowshipped with them did not represent the true Gospel. The authentic Gospel embraced freedom, justice, and mercy. In his Appeal, a document published in the late 1820s calling on the enslaved to rebel violently if necessary to attain their freedom, David Walker speaks of his great disappointment with whites in general, wondering at times if they might not be "natural enemies" of blacks. Regarding white Christians in particular, he lambasted those who practice a form of slavery worse than any ever witnessed on earth, including that of the Pharaoh of Egypt against the Hebrews and even that of contemporary "pagan" nations. How, then, could supporters of slavery dare go into other parts of the world and attempt to convert the unsaved to the Christian faith? Explicitly or implicitly, for Walker those who preach the gospel of freedom, including of course African American Christians, are the ones who will be most successful in passing the faith on to non-Christians. Furthermore, Walker boldly stated, God is on the side of the oppressed; the Divine One would not leave African Americans locked in the jaws of servitude. He foresaw a violent conflict that would divide the nation because of the evils of slavery. Robert Alexander Young, author of the *Ethiopian Manifesto*, prophesied the coming of a Messiah to deliver blacks from servitude. Nat Turner in his Southampton, Virginia, rebellion of 1831 understood himself as a deliverer commissioned by God to lead the great battle against the slaveholders.[9]

Enslaved African Americans, the vast majority of the

antebellum black population, also shared the view of the evils of slavery and of their special place in the providence of God. Many scholars of the black experience miss the very nature of black religion because they rely on documentation and records from white observers or white-controlled churches, often those supportive of slavery. Reading such materials, one might conclude that African Americans viewed whites as worthy Christians, that they depended upon white Christians for proper instructions in the faith, and that some type of strong Christian fellowship existed between white and black Christians. There is certainly some degree of truth in these statements, but many commentators have vastly overstated the case because they have not focused on the testimony of the enslaved themselves. As those black and white scholars who have focused more intensely on the experiences of the enslaved, such as Albert Raboteau and John Blassingame, have discovered, racism and slavery helped to solidify the enslaved understanding that as blacks they were one people, regardless of color variations, denominational affiliations, or their own status of enslavement or freedom.[10]

Studies of the "invisible institution," the network of religious beliefs, practices, and activities among the slaves that went largely unseen by whites, reveal that the enslaved claimed a clearer, more authentic understanding of the Christian faith than either their white oppressors or their sympathizers. Far from being brainwashed into accepting a "white man's religion," the Christian enslaved refused to believe chattel slavery or racial discrimination consistent with the will of God. Contrary to the popular myth that the enslaved were Christianized by whites, the truth is that Christianity passed from blacks and whites to blacks and whites: most of the enslaved embraced the faith through the ministry of other slaves. Given the nature of evangelical Protestantism, and its great emphasis on the responsibility and privilege of each saved individual to share the news with others, much of this spreading of Christianity among the enslaved came by way of laypeople, not ministers.

On a day-by-day basis, how did the enslaved deal with the question of theodicy as it applied to slavery? That is, how did they reconcile their faith in an all-powerful, just, and loving God with their experience of chattel slavery? The immediacy of God's presence, as when the Divine One appeared to Job, assured them of God's proximity and love. Identifying with Moses and the enslaved Hebrew people, Daniel in the lion's den, Paul and Silas, and of course Jesus himself offered comfort and the sense that God, despite harsh circumstances or perhaps because of them, was with God's people. They surely had faith that whatever the catastrophes and sufferings of this life, a righteous and loving God would vindicate them at death, granting eternal life to the faithful and punishing the sinful. Finally, enslaved Christians prayed earnestly for physical freedom in this life and firmly believed that such was coming. Surely God's judgment on the evils of American slavery and love for the faithful meant that God would soon act in history to free the oppressed.

EMANCIPATION, RECONSTRUCTION, JIM CROW, AND DIVINE PROVIDENCE

Their hopes were not in vain, and their prayers, they sincerely believed, were answered with the coming of the Civil War. We must not permit our contemporary ideologies and political agendas to obscure or minimize the significance and power of the experience of emancipation for enslaved blacks or their free kinspeople. Seeing how far the newly freed had to travel to full and equal American citizenship, and their subsequent experiences of Jim Crow segregation, disfranchisement, and poverty, later African American scholars and writers often lose sight of the depths of racist, chattel slavery and the shift in consciousness and meaning its abolition effected for even the most oppressed of the newly freed.[11] For example, William Jones queried black theologians in the late twentieth century regarding evidence that God had indeed acted in human history in a manner which demonstrated that the Divine One frees the oppressed.[12] Apparently they all missed the opportunity to cite the Emancipation Proclamation and the Thirteenth, Fourteenth, and Fifteenth Amendments to the Constitution. Surely all forms of oppression did not vanish with Emancipation—neither did all forms of suffering forever evaporate for the biblical Hebrews freed from Egyptian bondage—yet even in the worst of times the Jewish community has continued to celebrate the Passover and the conviction that God acts in history on behalf of the Chosen People.

However racist some of the white Union soldiers or equivocal the actions of northern white politicians might have been, the enslaved saw God's mighty hand in the Civil War delivering them from oppression. They believed that whatever human beings intended or did not intend, God still had a divine plan to work out and a providential people to deliver. For northern whites it was a Civil War, a rebellion on the part of white Southerners; for white Southerners it was a War for Southern Independence from the tyranny of Yankeedom. But for African Americans it was the War of Black Emancipation, bringing an end to chattel suffering and punishing a nation, North and South, that had permitted such a wrong to last so long. Along the way some African Americans forgot their earlier conviction that the Civil War was their Exodus experience, and with that loss they also experienced a diminution in confidence that God would again act on their behalf.

The Reconstruction Era, from roughly 1867 to 1877, continued this Exodus experience. As the fortunes of blacks slowly eroded (and this decline occurred gradually) from the demise of Reconstruction to the beginning of Jim Crowism and disfranchisement in the 1890s, African American Christian leaders still voiced confidence in the Black Christian Consensus and its belief that God had a providential plan for the race.[13] First, they emphasized that blacks had made great progress in education, land owner-ship, political participation, and in other ways since the days of chattel slavery and that they should continue to take full advantage of all available opportunities. Such hard work and dedication, such a display of moral charac-ter would demonstrate the ability and worth of blacks and empower them in whatever situation they found them-selves. Booker T. Washington's philosophy was perfectly consistent with, and in large part derived from, this Black Christian consensus, except that he, unlike the great ma-jority of black denominational leaders and with disastrous consequences, advanced the economic and moral aspects of the struggle at the expense of the political.

Second, some leaders understood the difficult days of racial proscription and terror as God's "scourging" of the race, testing it in the wilderness of renewed oppression, so that it might return to more faithful service. With their re-pentance from sinful ways and their steadfastness in the church, black Christians could expect that just as in the past, God would act in history to save them. Third, black religious leaders constantly reminded the people of better days ahead. On the one hand, these spokespersons might be criticized for being naive, unrealistic, and unmindful of the devastating effects of adverse economic, political, and social factors; on the other, a people must have hope or they become a major participant in their own destruction. In addition, these leaders trusted in God's providence and divine concern for a people with a special mission. In the most trying of times, they had unshakable faith in the ultimate triumph of God's will and the freedom of African Americans.

CHALLENGING THE
BLACK CHRISTIAN CONSENSUS

By the 1930s the public hegemony of Protestantism in American life had broken down, given the continued growth of non-Protestant denominations, augmented particularly by the increased immigration of European Catholics and Orthodox Christians and Jews into the United States beginning around the last quarter of the nineteenth century and extending into the first two decades of the twentieth. Similarly, from 1910 through the 1960s the Black Christian Consensus was also undergoing a great challenge because of a number of cultural, religious, and demographic factors.[14] The rise of blues, jazz, movies, the automobile, and freer sexual mores, among other things, contributed to a greater secularization and even a demoralization of African American life, just as it did among the general population. Increased urbanization (the Great Migration) beginning around 1915 moved considerable numbers of blacks from rural areas in the South to urban areas in the South and the North. In this new environment, with its greater emphasis on the individual and on personal life, church people did not enjoy the kind of intimate, social, kinship communities characteristic of the rural South. The growth of Holiness and Pentecostal churches in these urban areas as well as the rise of "storefront churches" (smaller congregations whose clergy had less formal training or fewer official connections to the major religious traditions) helped to retain the spirituality of the older rural churches, but changes wrought by urbanization proceeded.

Finally, new religious groups and movements proliferated, Father Divine, Daddy Grace, Moorish Science Temple, Nation of Islam, Church of God (Black Jews), and the Commandment Keepers, among others. Many of these movements offered radically new interpretations of religion, and some openly attacked the legitimacy of Christianity, which had particular implications for the historic Black Christian Consensus on the providential mission of the black race. To be sure, some of the Afro-Hebrew and Afro-Islamic groups did speak of God's providence, black identity, and the providential mission of African peoples. Often, however, their teachings were characterized by a racial chauvinism and exclusivism radically divorced from the traditional religious consciousness of African Americans, which might help explain why their memberships constituted such a small percentage of black religious people. Nevertheless, the activities of these groups helped to further estrange a larger number of blacks from Christianity, while not completely converting them, and thus undermined people's faith in God's providential mission for the race. All this occurred during years when many black Christian leaders, facing increased racial oppression and diminishing opportunities for leadership in the larger society, focused less on the providential destiny and purpose inherent in the Black Christian Consensus and more on the operational aspects of their denominations and the pursuit of their personal ecclesiastical-political ambitions.

Randall Burkett and others have pointed out the religious character and connections of the Marcus Garvey-led Pan-African movement, which extended in powerful ways into the 1920s. Certainly many mainstream black clergy and laypersons supported that movement.[15] But unlike the African mission movement, which incorporated strong Pan-African features, Garveyism did not receive the strong support or the official endorsement of the major black denominations. Despite its religious traits and ecclesial connections, it remained a largely secular or at least a quasi-secular movement. In addition, it placed emphasis on Africa as "home" and declared that black peoples under the government of whites would never achieve parity of opportunity and treatment. Unlike the Black Christian Consensus, Garveyism pointed black Americans toward a primary identity with a land beyond their first-hand knowledge and away from the hope of God's intervention in history to assist them in achieving full status as Americans. Clearly, by the early 1950s, the Consensus that African American Christians had a special role to play in history concomitant with their own liberation in the United States under the guiding hand of God, was eroding.

KING, BLACK NATIONALISM, AND THE BLACK CHRISTIAN CONSENSUS

Yet the Consensus retained a strong presence, and with the advent of Martin Luther King, Jr., and the modern Civil

Rights Movement in the mid-fifties, it witnessed a major revitalization.[16] Consistent with the historic Black Christian Consensus, the Civil Rights Movement mobilized the masses for a direct challenge to a system of racial oppression and inequality using the weapons of Christianity and the American Constitution. Blacks, in their quest for justice, were asked to be what the Consensus had always proclaimed—truly American and truly Christian. Rather than renounce their country and culture, Afro-Christians affirmed and struggled to perfect them. The movement understood the need for the salvation of the oppressed but not at the expense of the oppressor's redemption, whose reconciliation with God and humanity it sought. The issue was not black against white but good (supported by blacks and whites) against evil (injustice and racism). If all black churches did not vigorously support the Civil Rights Movement, they did not actively oppose it, the Reverend Joseph Harrison Jackson notwithstanding.

As Malcolm X (El-Hajj Malik El-Shabazz) moved from the racial provincialism of the Nation of Islam to a greater grasp of the sociopolitical situation of African peoples, he built a legacy of black nationalism that appealed to blacks beyond the boundaries of Islam.[17] The secular black nationalists of the late 1960s and early 1970s, to a great extent his political heirs, filled important gaps in the cultural and psychological thought and behavior of blacks left by the mainstream Civil Rights Movement. Black nationalism emphasized the value of the specific affirmation of blackness that was not lost in a vision of human universality, and it underscored the significance of black history and culture. At the same time, however, the secular black nationalist movement emphasized ideas that in connection with other factors contributed in the long run to a severe weakening of the Black Christian consensus. It advocated social action at the expense or neglect of personal morality (a trait that had begun with the Civil Rights Movement), not realizing that oppressed people in particular require a strong code of moral behavior to equip them for struggle and for just, equitable behavior once they attain their goals. The nationalists' attacks on Christian ministers and churches undercut their moral authority and stifled a stronger and more lasting renaissance of the Consensus.[18] Likewise, nationalists undermined confidence in the mainstream black leadership of groups such as the Southern Christian Leadership Conference, the National Association for the Advancement of Colored People, and the Urban League. Finally, with their explicit or implied hatred of or hostility toward whites, secular nationalists failed, with a philosophy often lacking in more pointedly spiritual and moral components, to accentuate the love of blacks for each other. Instead, once black nationalists had largely been killed, exiled, imprisoned, or bought off, black youth and succeeding generations were left without leadership they would accept, directing their anger and hatred toward each other or being led by it to nihilism.[19] The black nationalists de-Christianized the struggle and took away or obscured the sense of a black providential mission.

CONCLUDING THOUGHTS: HOPE FOR A REVITALIZED CONSENSUS?

At the dawn of the twenty-first century is there any hope of revitalizing a triumphant Black Christian consensus? Besides the Civil Rights Movement, two important developments within the last fifty years would seem to offer some hope, but both are characterized by limiting elements. The first is the religious and political thought of Joseph H. Jackson. Jackson, the president of the National Baptist Convention, USA, Incorporated, from the early 1950s to the early 1980s, offered a solid philosophy in theory, embracing the best of integrationism and separatism, and focused on Protestant Evangelical Christianity, the particularity of blackness within an integrated society, and economic development along with civic participation. But his disdain for King and the nonviolent resistance movement and his desire to retain ecclesial power alienated him from the socially active progressive tradition. The other hopeful development is the rise of Black Theology. This scholarly discourse, stating that the liberation of oppressed black people is at the heart of a true understanding and application of the Christian Gospel, has had a great impact beyond the walls of academia. Many ministers and informed laity may not overtly name themselves devotees of formal Black Theology as advocated by James H. Cone, J. Deotis Roberts, and Jacquelyn Grant. But its belief that the Christian gospel must have particular relevance to the social, economic, and political struggles of black people is consistent with the Civil Rights Movement and the historic Black Christian consensus, and has brought clarity and focus to many committed to the cause of Christ. Black Theology could more firmly secure its place in the consensus if it regained its focus on the primary task of liberating African Americans from the throes of racism, while concomitantly appropriating to itself the evangelical nature of Christianity. It must continue to champion gender equity, particularly in regard to black women, while affirming a more explicit commitment to the maintenance, strengthening, and growth of the heterosexually based, two-parent family. Conversely, it needs to reexamine its ideological commitment to socialism (democratic or otherwise) as the only pragmatic avenue for full liberation and, especially with a younger generation of Black Theologians, avoid the too comfortable embrace and affiliations with rap and hip-hop culture that often result in the promulgation of "low life" morality rather than, as intended, a liberative ethic for the lower socioeconomic class of our people.

In sum, this essay has attempted to outline the elements of black religious life that have contributed to and sustained the people's struggle for spiritual and temporal liberation. Two significant elements of what this essay has termed the Black Christian consensus are the abiding confidence that an all-wise, all-powerful, and all-loving God rules the universe and operates within history and the belief that black Americans, especially Afro-Christians, have a key role to play not only in attaining their own salvation but in contributing to the betterment of American society and the world. The loss of these elements in contemporary black secular and religious life, among other factors, has contributed to a stagnation in the perception of a sense of duty, significance, direction, and hope among black Americans. Any effort to liberate black people in the United States will be most successful in the near future if its objectives and operations are consistent with the historic Black Christian consensus.

EVIL &
SALVATION

Waymaking and Dimensions of Responsibility

An African American Perspective on Salvation

Genna Rae McNeil

IT IS of enormous significance that for centuries, countless African American Christians have affirmed "Salvation" as vitally connected with spaciousness, deliverance, rescue, liberation or freedom, consistent with the original Hebrew understanding of *yasha*.[1] Whether affirming ultimate salvation or pre-eschaton salvation, in the African American experience the nature of salvation is to provide space—psychic, physical, and spiritual—in which to function as a free being. As James Washington explained in *Frustrated Fellowship*, "those slaves . . . were trapped inside a social world that both absolved and deflected the values of the larger society."[2] Nevertheless, "the slaves and free blacks forged in the New World a new compact between their African cultural heritage and their need for a spiritual genealogy. This new religion provided psychic and spiritual sustenance for a people in the grip of oppression."[3]

Such sustenance incorporated a sense of options and access to what Michel de Certeau has called "the capacity for believing."[4] This facilitated "ways of operating" within a world in which the central fact of the bodily experience of blacks was racial oppression and/or slavery based upon African descent.[5] Expanding one's *Weltanschauung*, and as a consequence one's world, to include spiritual experiences that superseded physical bondage and limitation based upon race or color became a realizable possibility when introduced to Jesus as "the way and the truth, and the life."[6] Upon confession of faith and acceptance of Christian beliefs, African Americans—whether literate or unlettered, enslaved or free—understood God's identity in Psalm 46:1 ("God is our refuge and strength, a very present help in trouble") as a divine promise of space and deliverance, sufficiency, safety, and increased power. Yet they also recognized the experience of salvation through Christ Jesus as the promise of life in its fullness ("I am come that they might have life, and that they might have it more abundantly," John 10:10–18).

Enslaved and other racially oppressed Africans worked out a way in which to experience degrees of freedom even when familial relationships and other considerations prevented the enslaved from running away and the denizen from resisting discriminatory Black Laws. To be saved was to understand that even when one could not fully exercise physical freedom, one retained the option of exercising one's inner authority and thereby determining for oneself—informed by one's vision and God's promise—the significance one attached to one's life. "[T]here is one option that remains available. I can select the things against which I shall stand with my life and the things for which I shall stand,"[7] insisted Howard Thurman.

James Melvin Washington argued similarly. One of the functions of spirituality—and by implication, salvation—was "to provide us with privileged access to our own souls."[8] This is tantamount to a sufficient spiritual space in which to retain or assume through spiritual, emotional, and intellectual freedom an inner authority. It suggests one can retain or seize the power to define options and redefine circumstances, if one is willing to participate in the labor of spiritual disciplines after accepting salvation, a gift freely given by God.

Persons of African descent found and continue to find room to conduct themselves as free, morally responsible, spiritually empowered members of communities as well as creative ways to operate with a sense of spiritual freedom.[9] As Washington noted, "the founders of the black church movement were strong believers in religious freedom. They led black folk in affirming what they believed to be the natural, God-given right to freedom. But this was not a notion of freedom without responsibility. Souls had to be saved, brothers and sisters in bondage had to be liberated, churches had to be organized and built."[10]

Whether in the antebellum period, characterized by legal enslavement, or after the emancipation, many African Americans have taken seriously a sense of freedom by which God has opened and will continue to open a way for personal agency, despite confinement or wilderness situations.[11] Within the freedom provided by salvation, many African Americans have also embraced and continue to embrace the guidance and direction available because of the Incarnation. Not only can the Lord "make a way of no way," but the Lord *will* make a way and offer divine guidance through God's Word in prayer, preaching, and proclamation through music or testimony. The Word made flesh, Jesus Christ, can be understood as constantly teaching and guiding through example, lest one fall into doubt about which way to go. Reginald Hildebrand, in *The Times Were Strange and Stirring*, provides compelling evidence of the emergence of a "Gospel of Freedom" that privileged such an African American interpretation of salvation's fullest meaning and through its preaching by free Black ministers nurtured a multiplicity of ways of operating as empowered, unconfined persons.[12]

Too often, for African Americans in the United States the reality has been one of closed doors as well as blocked passageways, physical and psychic assaults, or pathless journeys. Necessarily, understandings of salvation have been contextual as well as theological. Race has become so important in this nation that, as James Washington observed, "you are engaged in an idolatrous situation."[13] The social construction of race serves as one of the primary categories of identification in the United States. "Whiteness" has become so consistently associated with the good, right, and beautiful by holders of power and much of the white majority that reverence for it is systemically rewarded. To be Other may mean that one experiences a wide range of forms of objectification (e.g., from stereotyping to demonization). For far too many, whiteness is that which places one above others or is a goal to be achieved if one is to be valued and to succeed. Conversely, the majority, in language and conduct, devalues blackness, often associating it with that which is to be shunned or that which is inferior and/or evil. Veneration of a superior racial classification has confounded, in some cases, and trivialized or subjected to derision, in others, practices that would reserve worship, adoration, and ultimate reverence for a supernatural deity. Indeed, the belief in white supremacy has become "a spiritual problem."[14]

Nevertheless, at the level of its most profound meaning, Washington understood and believed salvation constituted the basis for an inextinguishable hope. Salvation encompassed the fundamental, profound truth not only of a redeemable past, but also of the most comprehensive liberation in the human's physical, emotional, mental, and spiritual experiences.

James Washington believed that the hope offered by Christianity and salvation could be uniquely understood by examining the African American experience, and that in so doing anyone might gain insight into both spirituality and the meaning of Christianity. Fundamentally, he posited through his life and work that when the hope of the Christian faith is viewed from an African American perspective it renders salvation a gift, a legacy, and a responsibility. That it is the gift of God through grace as proclaimed in John 3:16 and Ephesians 2:5 and not something persons could become worthy enough to earn was essential to the traditional African American interpretation of scripture, to preaching, testimonies, and prayers. Yet the legacy of African American Christianity is a perspective on salvation that continually challenges the believer to know the dimensions of responsibility consistent with expressing gratitude for the gift.

There is a vital connection between yielding one's consent to God, belief in an omnipotent God whose deeds are providential, and the hope of salvation. For God's professing believers, faith means an active commitment to hope. This recognition grows out of the essential message of the salvific event. Howard Thurman's description is telling:

> there is a Spirit at work in life and in the hearts of men
> which is committed to overcoming the world. It is universal, knowing no age, no race, no culture, and no condi-

tion of men. For the privileged and underprivileged
alike, if the individual puts at the disposal of the Spirit
the needful dedication and discipline, he can live effectively in the chaos of the present the high destiny of a
son of God.[15]

Despite historical research that confirmed the idolatry
of so many and the daily incursions of not only the absurd
but also the demonic, a hope of salvation at many levels
permitted James Washington to affirm that

> Every minute of each fleeting day documents how hu-
> man forgetfulness ends with someone's death, or is di-
> minished by someone's birth. Children who have not
> been captured by the cynicisms of adulthood replenish
> the imagination of the human community. My personal
> experience and historical research have taught me that
> the children of God, when at their best, also inspire the
> best in us.[16]

African American ancestors could not accept God's gift
of salvation without recognizing the challenge it presented
in regard to one's perspective on human possibility. Salvation became and becomes responsibility as well as gift because the grace by which anyone is saved is, as Dietrich
Bonhoeffer described it, "costly grace."[17] Having cost God
an only son to establish the opportunity for hope and everlasting life, what African American Christians transmitted
from one generation to the next was a radical, challenging
hope. Salvation as a gift available to all—regardless of race,
sex, or class—underscored what Samuel DeWitt Proctor
called a permanent "margin of freedom" and Howard
Thurman described as the ever-present "growing edge."[18]
For Proctor this salvation through Christ shows us the
"freedom available . . . to rise above the past . . . [to] that
inner sanctuary of the soul . . . where we have some power
to choose. . . . 'I can do all things . . . through Christ.' "[19]

For Thurman this was the unshakable belief that "no experience, no event at any particular moment in time or space exhausts what life is trying to do"; there ought not be the sinking down of "our hopes and our dreams and our yearnings to the level of the event of our lives."[20] Salvation then, challenges each believer to assume responsibility for self and nurture within the society. Living one's faith and transmitting the message of salvation are part and parcel of recognizing one's responsibility for human nurture. Through control of nurture, Washington insisted, you expand or "you limit the *possibility of possibility*. And the spiritual vision of whatever faith . . . is the chance that there's an alternative cosmology."[21]

Salvation is understood as the commitment to the possibility of human community in which persons acknowledge a God of love and justice, which makes possible our living within the tensions of Otherness and common creaturehood with humility and hope, as well as faith. Washington's life and work substantiated several meanings of hope in relation to acceptance of the gift of salvation from an African American Christian perspective. To accept the gift of salvation is to live in the full knowledge and unassailable belief that after Jesus' ministry, crucifixion, and resurrection, no human act can forever eradicate the *possibility of possibility*. To accept the gift of salvation is to live in the full knowledge and unassailable belief that after Jesus' ministry, crucifixion, and resurrection, no human act is the last word on or work of love and justice. The God of salvation will ultimately disclose not only the ascendancy and vindication of love and justice, but also God's ultimate authority and victory. This core belief nurtured the hope resident and triumphant in salvation.

James Melvin Washington counseled and preached obedience to the author of salvation; this entailed both bold
actions and patient, faithful waiting. The hope of salvation
affirmed that for the believer there is an overcoming already accomplished wherein, in scorn of the apparent
overwhelming evidence of suffering and evil, we may see
our lives from a spiritual perspective. This means that having "privileged access to our souls" prevents our permanent embracing of a conclusion that our human striving
and our spiritual disciplines are meaningless. Washington
consistently preached that the hope consistent with obeying Christ, yielding to God, and believing in the efficacy of
the promise of salvation required the saved to face history
as well as the excesses and evils of society with solemn dec-
larations. First, "God gets no pleasure out of watching our
pain. God is a God who cares. That's why the writer cried
out: 'For God so loved the world that He gave his only be-
gotten son (all He had) that whosoever shall believe . . . in
Him shall not perish, but shall have everlasting life.' [John
3:16] God cares. Pain has a function. . . . It is a warning:
'do something.' "[22]

Second, James Washington understood salvation to justify the declaration that "God deserves your patience.
You've got to learn how to be patient with God. Isaiah
cried out: 'They that wait upon the Lord shall renew their
strength. They shall mount up with wings as eagles. They
shall run and not be weary. They shall walk and not faint.' "
Lest there be confusion about the meaning of "waiting
upon the Lord," Washington further explained: "Waiting
is a sacrament. It is a discipline. It is not some namby-
pamby acquiescence. It is about learning how to hang in
there tough with love, even when it seems there is not evi-

dence."[23] When salvation can be viewed as the source of a deeply rooted and faith-based hope, an African American historical perspective illuminating the gift, legacy, and responsibility of salvation validates a defiant hope. "You don't have to be confined to what the world tells you is reality," and "there is the possibility of reconceiving oneself," as well as participating in the transformation of human community. Even when waiting, salvation places one squarely in the process of the transformation activity, what James Washington has also called "the cosmology-lifting-up business."[24]

This essay has argued for an African American interpretation of salvation explicit and implicit in the life and work of James Melvin Washington.[25] Critical examination of an African American Christian concept of salvation historically, contextually, and culturally construed affirms the notion of African American Christianity as an inexhaustible resource for the sustenance of African American people. Washington wrote as if to elucidate African American spirituality by both subverting and expanding common understandings of the grounds for hope and the basis for the assertion of one's possession of freedom and power. Examining specific folk beliefs, theological musings, and lived faith actions, Washington uncovered multiple meanings of salvation in the African American experience. An experience effective and empowering beyond discourse or even testimony, such salvation included (and includes) three critical elements.[26]

First, salvation is a revolutionary spaciousness and freedom through the assertion of inner authority, breaking bonds of confinement and invalidating the reality of dead-ends. To have salvation is to know through experience and faith that God will "make a way out of no way." Having salvation, ironically, requires that one be ever cognizant of one's inner authority yet ultimately establish one's freedom in this world by refusing to yield the central source of one's personal consent to anyone or anything other than God, the author of salvation. It is to know God as deliverer and waymaker.

Second, to be saved is to have engaged in dissent and resistance. Defiant seizing of psychic space characterizes the free, saved believer. It is to understand a particular set of meanings for salvation in regard to the mind. To receive salvation as a freely given inheritance for the children of God is to "be clothed in one's right mind" and know the ultimate mind-regulator, who is God. This not only lifts the spirit and mind, but establishes peace of mind, depth, and breadth congruent with God's grace, love, and forgiveness. It is as well however, to yield the nerve center of consent to the highest authority, faithfully believing this the best choice. Having salvation is to transpose terrors, absurdities, angst, depression, and all manner of external and mental demons into a response to God that is new harmonious song.

Third, salvation is and sustains an abiding knowledge and confident expectation that ultimately the end of one's earthly striving and waiting will be a "win/win" situation. In the salvific event, the triune God prevailed over ultimate bondage, loss, defeat, nihilism and despair. All these— when one waits upon the Lord in the sense of the spiritual discipline—become temporary setbacks and fleeting feelings, ultimately more illusory than real. To be saved is to live acknowledging the reality of infinite creative possibilities, the inexhaustibility of hope, and a divine invitation for all persons—regardless of race, class or sex—to experience everlasting life.

The last word must be James Melvin Washington's. Hear the prayer of this believer, confident of his salvation and its author, God.

> O Lord, we need you today. We know you're able. We know that you know us better than we know ourselves. We know you've got the power to make *a way out of no way*, understanding in the midst of confusion, power in the midst of weakness. O Lord, help us this day. Somebody came, came out to your house of worship today because *there is a promise* that you are able to deliver us from all that befalls us. We trust in you today because we know that *you are a waymaker*, a burden-bearer, a friend beyond all friends, a great deliverer. We know this day that whatever, *whatever* falls upon us, that it's all in your hands. . . . We ask you this day to bless us, to keep us, to lead us, to guide us, to show us *a way out of no way,* our help in the time of trouble. In the wilderness we need to find our way home.[27]

"CALLING THE OPPRESSORS TO ACCOUNT"

Justice, Love, and Hope in Black Religion

James H. Cone

> God is not dead,—nor is he an indifferent onlooker at what is
> going on in this world. One day He will make requisition for
> blood; He will call the oppressors to account. Justice may
> sleep, but it never dies. The individual, race, or nation which
> does wrong, which sets at defiance God's great law, especially
> God's great law of love, of brotherhood, will be sure, sooner
> or later, to pay the penalty. We reap as we sow. With what
> measure we mete, it will be measured to us again.

THIS 1902 statement by Francis Grimke,[1] an ex-slave
and Princeton Theological Seminary graduate, is an
apt summary of the major themes of justice, hope, and love
in African American religion from slavery to the present.
These themes were created out of the African slaves' encounter with biblical religion (via white missionaries and
preachers) as they sought to make meaning in a strange
world. To make meaning in any world is difficult because
human beings, like other animals, are creatures of nature
and history. We can never be what we can imagine, but to
be slaves in a foreign land without the cultural and religious support of a loving family and a caring community
limits human possibilities profoundly. Because Africans
were prevented from freely practicing their native religion,
they merged their knowledge of their cultural past with the
white man's Christian religion. From these two sources,

Africans created for themselves a world of meaning that enabled them to survive 244 years of slavery and 100 years of segregation—augmented by a reign of white terror that lynched more than five thousand black people.

The black religious themes of justice, hope, and love are the product of black people's search for meaning in a white society that did not acknowledge their humanity. The most prominent theme in this trinity of divine virtues is the justice of God. Faith in God's righteousness is the starting point of black religion. African Americans have always believed in the living presence of the God who establishes the right by punishing the wicked and liberating their victims from oppression. Everyone will be rewarded and punished according to their deeds, and no one—absolutely no one—can escape the judgment of God, who alone is the sovereign of the universe. Evildoers may get by for a time, and good people may suffer unjustly under oppression, but "sooner or later, . . . we reap as we sow."

The "sooner" referred to contemporary historically observable events: punishment of the oppressors and liberation of the oppressed. The "later" referred to the divine establishment of justice in the "next world," where God "gwineter rain down fire" on the wicked and where the liberated righteous will "walk in Jerusalem just like John." In the religion of African slaves, God's justice was identical with the punishment of the oppressors, and divine liberation was synonymous with the deliverance of the oppressed from the bondage of slavery—if not "now" then in the "not yet." Because whites continued to prosper materially as they increased their victimization of African Americans, black religion spoke more often of the "later" than the "sooner."

The theme of justice is closely related to the idea of hope. The God who establishes the right and puts down the wrong is the sole basis of the hope that the suffering of the victims will be eliminated. Although African slaves used the term heaven to describe their experience of hope, its primary meaning for them must not be reduced to the "pie-in-the sky," otherworldly affirmation that often characterized white evangelical Protestantism. The idea of heaven was the means by which slaves affirmed their humanity in a world that did not recognize them as human beings. It was their way of saying that they were made for freedom and not slavery.

> *Oh Freedom! Oh Freedom!*
> *Oh Freedom, I love thee!*
> *And before I'll be a slave,*
> *I'll be buried in my grave,*
> *And go home to my Lord and be free.*

Black slaves' hope was based on their faith in God's promise to "protect the needy" and to "defend the poor." Just as God delivered the Hebrew children from Egyptian bondage and raised Jesus from the dead, so God will also deliver African slaves from American slavery and "in due time" will bestow upon them the gift of eternal life. That was why they sang:

> *Soon-a-will be done with the trouble of this world;*
> *Soon-a-will be done with the trouble of this world;*
> *Going home to live with God.*

Black slaves' faith in the coming justice of God was the chief reason they could hold themselves together in servitude and sometimes fight back, even though the odds were against them.

The ideas of justice and hope should be seen in relation to the important theme of love. Theologically God's love is prior to the other themes. But in order to separate love in the context of black religion from a similar theme in white religion, it is important to emphasize that love in black religion is usually linked with God's justice and hope. God's love is made known through divine righteousness, liberating the poor for a new future.

God's creation of all persons in the divine image bestows sacredness upon human beings and thus makes them the children of God. To violate any person's dignity is to transgress "God's great law of love." We must love our neighbor because God has first loved us. And because slavery and segregation are blatant denials of the dignity of the human person, divine justice means God "will call the oppressors to account."

Despite the strength of black faith, belief in God's coming justice and liberation was not easy for African slaves and their descendants. Their continued suffering created the most serious challenge to their faith. If God is good, why did God permit millions of blacks to be stolen from Africa, perish in the Middle Passage, and enslaved in a strange land? No black person has been able to escape the existential agony of that question.

In their attempt to resolve the theological dilemma that slavery and segregation created, African Americans in the nineteenth century turned to two texts: Exodus and Psalm 68:31. They derived from the Exodus text the belief that God is the liberator of the oppressed. They interpreted Psalm 68:31 as an obscure reference to God's promise to redeem Africa: "Princess shall come out of Egypt, and Ethiopia shall soon stretch forth her hands unto God." Despite African Americans' reflections on these texts, contradictions remained between their sociopolitical oppression and their religious faith.

Throughout the twentieth century African Americans continued their struggle to reconcile their faith in the justice and love of God with the persistence of black suffering in the land of their birth. Writer James Baldwin expressed the feelings of most African Americans: "If [God's] love was so great, and if He loved all His children, why were we, the blacks, cast down so far?"[2] It was Martin Luther King, Jr., a twenty-six-year-old Baptist preacher, who confronted the evil of white supremacy and condemned it as the greatest moral evil in American society. He organized a movement that broke the backbone of legal segregation in the South. From the beginning of his role as the leader of the yearlong Montgomery, Alabama, bus boycott (1955–56) to his tragic death in Memphis, Tennessee (April 4, 1968), Martin King was a public embodiment of the ideas of love, justice, and hope. The meaning of each was dependent on the others. Though love may be placed appropriately at the center of King's faith, he interpreted it in the light of justice for the poor, liberation for all, and the certain hope that God has not left this world in the hands of evil men.

Martin King took the American democratic tradition of freedom and combined it with the biblical tradition of liberation and justice as found in Exodus and the prophets. Then he integrated both traditions with the New Testament idea of love and hope as disclosed in Jesus' cross and resurrection. From these three sources, King developed a radical practice of nonviolence that was effective in challenging all Americans to create the beloved community in which all persons are equal. While it was Gandhi's method of nonviolence that provided the strategy for achieving justice, it was, as King said, "through the influence of the Negro Church" that "the way of nonviolence became an integral part of our struggle."[3]

As a Christian whose faith was derived from the cross of Jesus, Martin King believed that there could be no true liberation without suffering. Through nonviolent suffering, he contended, blacks would not only liberate themselves from the necessity of bitterness and a feeling of inferiority toward whites, they would also prick the conscience of whites and liberate them from a feeling of superiority. The mutual liberation of blacks and whites lays the foundation for both to work together toward the creation of an entirely new world.

In accordance with this theological vision, King initially rejected black power because of its connotations of revenge, hate, and violence. He believed that no beloved community of blacks and whites could be created out of bitterness. Only love, which he equated with nonviolence, can create justice. When black power militants turned away from nonviolence and openly preached self-defense and violence, King said that he would continue to preach nonviolence even if he became its only advocate.

He took a similar position regarding the war in Vietnam. In the tradition of the Hebrew prophets and against the advice of his closest associates in black and white communities, King stood before a capacity crowd at Riverside Church on April 4, 1967, and condemned America as "the greatest purveyor of violence in the world today."[4] He proclaimed God's judgment against America and insisted that

God would break the backbone of U.S. power if this nation did not bring justice to the poor and peace to the world.

During the crises of 1967–68, King turned to his own religious heritage for strength to keep on fighting for justice and for the courage to face the certain possibility of his own death. "It doesn't matter with me now," King proclaimed in a sermon the night before his assassination, "because I've been to the mountaintop . . . and I've seen the Promised Land."[5] It was the eschatological hope, derived from his slave grandparents and mediated through the black church, which sustained him in the midst of the trials and tribulations in the black freedom struggle. He combined the justice and love themes in the prophets and the cross with the message of hope in the resurrection of Jesus. Hope for King was based on his belief in the righteousness of God as defined by his reading of the Bible through the eyes of his slave foreparents. The result was one of the most powerful faith responses to the theodicy question in African American history.

> Centuries ago Jeremiah raised the question, "Is there no balm in Gilead? Is there no physician?" He raised it because he saw the good people suffering so often and the evil people prospering. Centuries later our slave foreparents came along and they too saw the injustice of life and had nothing to look forward to, morning after morning, but the rawhide whip of the overseer, long rows of cotton and the sizzling heat; but they did an amazing thing. They looked back across the centuries, and they took Jeremiah's question mark and straightened it into an exclamation point. And they could sing, "There is a balm in Gilead to make the wounded whole. There is a balm in Gilead to heal the sin-sick soul."[6]

From the time of its origin in slavery to the present, black religion has been faced with the question of whether to advocate integration into American society or separation from it. The majority of the participants in the black churches and the civil rights movement have promoted integration, and they have interpreted justice, hope and, love in the light of the goal of creating a society in which black and white can live together in a beloved community.

While integrationists emphasized the American side of the identify of African Americans, black nationalists rejected any association with the United States and instead turned toward Africa. Nationalists contended that blacks will never be accepted as equals in a white racist church and society. Black freedom can be achieved only by blacks separating themselves from whites—either by returning to Africa or by forcing the U.S. government to set aside a separate territory in the United States so blacks can build their own society.

The nationalist perspective on the black struggle for justice is deeply embedded in the history of black religion. Some of its proponents include Martin Delaney, often called the founder of black nationalism; Marcus Garvey, the founder of the Universal Negro Improvement Association; and Malcolm X of the religion of Islam. Black nationalism was centered on blackness and saw no value in white culture and religion.

The most persuasive interpreter of black nationalism during the 1960's was Malcolm X, who proclaimed a challenging critique of Martin King's philosophy of integration, nonviolence, and love. Malcolm advocated black unity instead of the beloved community, self-defense in lieu of nonviolence, and self-love in place of turning the other cheek to whites.

Malcolm X rejected Christianity as the white man's religion. He became a convert initially to Elijah Muhammad's Nation of Islam and later to the worldwide Islamic community. His critique of Christianity and American society as white was so persuasive that many blacks followed him into the religion of Islam, and others accepted his criticisms even though they did not become Muslims. Malcolm pushed civil rights leaders to the left and caused many black Christians to reevaluate their interpretation of Christianity.

> Brothers and sisters, the white man has brainwashed us black people to fasten our gaze upon a blond-haired, blue-eyed Jesus! We're worshiping a Jesus that doesn't even *look* like us! Now just think of this. The blond-haired, blue-eyed white man has taught you and me to worship a *white* Jesus, and to shout and sing and pray to this God that's *his* God, the white man's God. The white man has taught to shout and sing and pray until we *die*, to wait until *death*, for some dreamy heaven-in-the-here-after, when we're *dead*, while this white man has his milk and honey in the streets paved with golden dollars right here on *this* earth![7]

During the first half of the 1960s, Martin King's interpretation of justice as equality with whites, liberation as integration, and love as nonviolence dominated the thinking of the black religious community. However, after the riot in Watts (Los Angeles, August 1965), some black religious activists began to take another look at Malcolm X's philosophy, especially in regard to his criticisms of Christianity and American society. Malcolm X's contention that America was a nightmare and not a dream began to ring true to many black clergy as they watched their communities go up in flames.

The rise of black power in 1966 created a decisive turning point in black religion. Black power forced black clergy to raise the theological question about the relation between black faith and white religion. Although blacks have always recognized the ethical heresy of white Christians ("Everybody talking about heaven ain't going there?") they have not always extended their race critique to Euro-American theology. With its accent on the cultural heritage of Africa and political liberation "by any means necessary," black power shook black religious leaders out of their theological complacency.

Separating themselves from Martin King's absolute commitment to nonviolence, a small group of black clergy, mostly from the North, addressed black power positively and critically. Like King and unlike black power advocates, black clergy were determined to remain within the Christian community. This was their dilemma: How could they reconcile Christianity and black power, Martin King and Malcolm X?

Under the influence of Malcolm X and the political philosophy of black power, many black theologians began to advocate for the development of a black theology. They rejected the dominant theologies of Europe and North America as heretical. For the first time in the history of black religion, black clergy and theologians began to recognize the need for a completely new starting point in theology, and they insisted that it must be defined by people at the bottom, not from the top of the socioeconomic ladder. To accomplish this task, black theologians focused on God's liberation of the poor as the central message of the gospel.

To explicate the theological significance of the liberation motif, black theologians began to reread the Bible through the eyes of their slave grandparents and started to speak of God's solidarity with the wretched of the earth. As the political liberation of the poor emerged as the dominant motif, justice, love, and hope were reinterpreted in its light. For the biblical meaning of liberation, black theologians turned to the Exodus, while the message of the prophets provided the theological content for the theme of justice. The gospel story of the life, death, and resurrection of Jesus served as the biblical foundation for a reinterpretation of love, suffering, and the hope in the context of the black struggle for liberation and justice.

There are many blacks, however, who find no spiritual or intellectual consolation in the Christian answer to the problem of theodicy. After nearly four hundred years of black presence in what is now known as the United States of America, black people still have to contend with white supremacy in every segment of their lives. This evil is so powerful and pervasive that no blacks can escape it. But poor blacks bear the heaviest brunt of it. The persistence of racism makes the creation of meaning difficult for blacks inside and outside the church.

Is God still going to call the oppressors to account? If so, when? Black churches seem to have no meaningful answer to these questions. They simply repeat worn-out religious cliches: "All things work out for the good for them who love the Lord." Black suffering in America and throughout the world, however, seems to be a blatant contradiction of that faith claim. No people are more religious than blacks. We faithfully attend churches and other religious services, giving reverence and love to the One who called us into being. But how long must black people wait for God to call our oppressors to account?

Black and womanist theologians have no satisfactory answers for the theodicy question either—at least not for those blacks looking for the meaning of our long struggle for justice. We can talk about God's justice and love from now to the end of time. But until our theological discourse engages white supremacy in a way that empowers poor people to fight the monster, then our theology is not worth the paper it is written on.

In 1903 W. E. B. Du Bois said: "The problem of the twentieth century is the problem of the color-line,—the relation of the darker to the lighter races of men in Asia and Africa, in America and the islands of the sea."[8] That message is as true today as it was when he uttered it. There is still no justice in the land for black people. "No justice, no peace" proclaimed blacks to whites during the 1992 Los Angeles riot. "No love, no justice" was Martin King's way of proclaiming to all who would listen. King's words are what whites want to hear when there is a racial disturbance in the black community. But African Americans want to know whether there is any reason to hope that the twenty-first century will be any less racist than the previous four centuries. Is there any reason to hope that we will be able to create a truly just society where justice and love flow freely between whites and blacks and among all peoples of the earth? Let us hope that enough people will bear witness to justice and love so as to inspire others to believe that with God and the practice of freedom fighters, "all things are possible."

DIFFERENCE AS EVIL

Judith Weisenfeld

THE CHARGE of reflecting on the topic of evil for my contribution to this collection has proven a profoundly paralyzing task for a number of reasons. It seems clear to me that most commonsense concepts of evil imply a theological context in which ultimate good is located in a divine presence and against which evil, immoral, and generally negative forces operate. As an ardent secularist, I find the notion of abstract evil forces implausible, to say the least, and I do not recognize a divine force as the primary agent in human history. I do not believe in an ultimate power that requires a single way of being in the world or that proscribes modes of worship or even sets the rhythm of daily life. I do have some faith, however, that people will make community where they can, and that in the making of bonds of community lies great merit—something that makes us more than we think we are precisely because it requires that we think beyond ourselves. Indeed, I find it tremendously compelling when people create community and connect with one another without the imposition of external motivators such as religious systems that seek to order one's life. And I am even more inspired when that community is not determined by commitment to a focused set of beliefs to the exclusion of anything outside the bounds of those beliefs. So even as it is the mundane level of human connections or disconnections that interests me considerably more than a cosmic battle between good and evil, I teach about religion in America because I recognize its power as one of the mechanisms through which people sometimes make community, as well as its function as a source of fundamental divisions among individuals and communities.

Conversations with friends and colleagues concerning this piece helped me to turn away from an approach dependent upon theological assertions about the source or direction of an intangible evil agent toward a focus on social constructions of the nature of evil in the American context and gradually lifted my initial paralysis.[1] Working to situate ideas about what constitutes evil in history provides a means to explore some of the ways in which these constructions militate against certain kinds of human connections and against the pursuit of knowledge about people different from ourselves. Here I am interested in the social implications of constructions of evil—that is, what happens because of a persistent unwillingness to attempt to view the world in ways that go beyond the easy and limited range of vision of the individual life.

We each live within a web of interconnected constituent elements of individual and communal identity—components such as race, gender, and sexuality—which do not represent "natural," eternal, or fixed ways of being, but which have emerged as ways of understanding people and their relationships across time and space. And, most significantly, it must be remembered that these concepts, which serve to order people in social contexts, develop largely through expressions of power. The idea of "race," for example, emerges when groups invest inconsequential physical differences between peoples with determinations of intellectual, physical, and moral capacity. Such understandings of the value of difference insist on a hierarchy stemming from these inherently incidental distinctions.[2] David Hume, for example, considered the implications of the "natural" distinctions between peoples in a 1748 essay entitled "Of National Characters," asserting "I am apt to suspect the negroes, and in general all the other species of men (for there are four or five different kinds) to be naturally inferior to the whites. There never was a civilized nation of any other complexion than white, nor even any individual eminent either in action or speculation. . . . Such a uniform and constant difference could not happen, in so many countries and ages, if nature had not made an original distinction betwixt these breeds of men."[3] The Georgia slaveholder and clergyman Charles Colcock Jones helped to formulate American ideas about race in his 1842 treatise *Religious Instruction of the Negroes in the United States.* His intervention on the subject of the relationship between religion and race came at a time when many aspects of the template had already been clearly set out, but it contributed to the ongoing process of shaping race. In this tract Jones engaged in debate those white Christian slaveholders who refused to extend the umbrella of Christian brotherhood to enslaved African Americans in the belief that religious instruction "ruined" them and incited rebellion. Jones countered this belief by reflecting on the relationship between white slaveholders and enslaved African Americans in ways that represent much of the discourse on religion, race, and slavery among white Americans in the antebellum South:

> At the head of the varieties of the human race, stands *the fair, or Caucasian variety*; "which," to use the language of another, "has given birth to the most civilized nations of ancient and modern times, and has exhibited the

moral and intellectual powers of human nature in their
highest degree of perfection." At the foot, stands *the
black or Ethiopian variety*, "which has ever remained in
a rude and barbarous state; and been looked upon and
treated as inferior by all the other varieties of the human
race, from time immemorial."[4]

Josiah Nott, in his 1844 address *Two Lectures on the Natural History of the Caucasian and Negro Races*, went so far as to assert—using both "scientific" and biblical sources—that the various peoples of the world must derive from entirely separate creations because he sees Anglo-Saxons as so far superior to other peoples. He wrote, "The unity of the human race is spoken of so seldom in the New Testament, and in such a passing way as to leave room for rational doubts on the subject; we are therefore at liberty to appeal to facts."[5] After considerable convoluted and torturous reasoning, Nott concluded, "The white and black races are now living together in the United States under circumstances which, if we may judge by the signs of the times cannot endure always, and it is time for the Philanthropist to do as I have done, look the question boldly in the face. What future course will be the wisest and most humane, I must leave to wiser heads than mine; but of this I am convinced, that nothing *wise can be done* without giving due weight to the *marked differences* which exist between the races."[6] Nott's protests aside, these men do not merely mark difference, but rather invest it with significant evaluations of moral and intellectual capacity and thereby construct the categories of race operative in the American context across long periods of our history.[7] Thus, *we* create race and live inside its structures, and *it*, in turn, creates us and profoundly shapes how we understand ourselves and the world around us.

Within the range of ideas about race, the production of

which necessarily entails formulating hierarchical interpretations of benign differences, the persistent association
of blackness with evil constitutes another layer of social
construction. Indeed, race and racial hierarchy rely upon
such associations, and the very notion of what constitutes
evil is itself created through this identification. Various
writers, in their endeavor to oppose a racial hierarchy in
which people of African descent inevitably remain at the
bottom, have noted the destructive power of the identification of blackness with evil. Toni Morrison goes beyond
merely noting the associations between blackness and evil
and its consequences, to focus on the flexibility of the
trope of the "American Africanism," as she calls it. She
writes of its uses in American literature:

> I use the term for the denotative and connotative black-
> ness that African peoples have come to signify, as well as
> the entire range of views, assumptions, readings, and
> misreadings that accompany Eurocentric learning about
> these people. As a trope, little restraint has been attached
> to its uses. As a disabling virus within literary discourse,
> Africanism has become, in the Eurocentric tradition that
> American education favors, both a way of talking about
> and a way of policing matters of class, sexual license, and
> repression, formations and exercises of power, and medi-
> tations on ethics and accountability. Through the simple
> expedient of demonizing and reifying the range of color
> on a palette, American Africanism makes it possible to
> say and not say, to inscribe and erase, to escape and en-
> gage, to act out and act on, to historicize and render time-
> less. It provides a way of contemplating chaos and civili-
> zation, desire and fear, and a mechanism for testing the
> possibilities and blessings of freedom.[8]

Thus, along with many others, I argue that the ideas about
race within which we operate depend profoundly on the

insistence that some races are "evil" and some are blessed and, indeed, destined to rule. Charles Colcock Jones drew such a conclusion:

> There is superiority on the one hand and inferiority on the other. Ascribe it to whatever cause you may; whether to the immediate providence of God, or to nature itself— to a difference in original constitution, or to circumstances; the fact remains, and it can but be seen and felt. It is only with *the fact*, and its influence on us, that we have to do. . . . What renders the superiority more palpable and influential in our case in the South, is that we still continue to maintain the relation of *master*, and all the *differences* in our standing privileges, and circumstances in society, created by that relation, in custom and in law. There is, consequently, superiority on the one side and inferiority on the other, in almost every point of view.[9]

Jones argues for certain duties that the divinely ordained social and moral position of master requires of white slaveholders and, in this regard, also participates in the powerful and profoundly racialized American discourse of crucibles and destinies. This discourse positions a particular group as God's chosen and covenanted people—and many groups have laid claim to this identity—and situates America as a site of both the purifying crucible of suffering and the literal location of the fulfillment of God's promises to his chosen. We can see the roots of the formulation of white, Christian American destiny in examples such as John Winthrop's famous 1630 sermon aboard the *Arbella*, en route to New England. Winthrop imagined the future of these sojourners as God's people, telling his listeners:

> The Lord will be our God, and delight to dwell among us, as his own people, and will command a blessing

upon us in all our ways. So that we shall see much more
of his wisdom, power, goodness and truth, than formerly
we have been acquainted with. We shall find that the
God of Israel is among us, when ten of us shall be able to
resist a thousand of our enemies; when he shall make us
a praise and glory that men shall say of succeeding plantations, "the Lord make it likely that of New England."
For we must consider that we shall be as a city upon a
hill. The eyes of all people are upon us.[10]

In such a view, the prosperity of the nation and Americans'
ability to vanquish enemies surely indicates the nation's
chosen status. Other white Christians, like Josiah Strong,
pursued this line of thinking in clearly racialized terms,
searching for signs of Anglo-Saxon destiny through the
development and expansion of America. Strong wrote in
1886,

Is it manifest that the Anglo-Saxon holds in his hands
the destinies of mankind for ages to come? Is it evident
that the United States is to be the home of this race,
the principal seat of his power, the great center of his
influence? . . . Notwithstanding the great perils which
threaten it, I cannot think our civilization will perish;
but I believe it is fully in the hands of the Christians of
the United States . . . to hasten or retard the coming of
Christ's kingdom in the world by hundreds, and perhaps
thousands of years.[11]

Where Winthrop's sermon does not give clear evidence of
a conviction that white Christian American chosenness depends on defeating the evil inherent in people of color,
Strong and others do make this significant connection and
establish a theological template that still functions today.

We see the most extreme version of the discourses of chosenness based on race in the theology of Christian white
supremacists today, particularly those associated with the
Christian Identity movement. Contemporary Christian

Identity theologians assert the natural supremacy of white peoples and understand people of color as merely inferior beings to be ignored or as entities whose presence in the world constitutes a test for God's chosen people. The movement's doctrinal statement begins:

> WE BELIEVE the White, Anglo-Saxon, Germanic and kindred people to be God's true, literal Children of Israel. Only this race fulfills every detail of Biblical Prophecy and World History concerning Israel and continues in these latter days to be heirs and possessors of the Covenants, Prophecies, Promises and Blessings YHVH God made to Israel. This chosen seedline making up the "Christian Nations" of the earth stands far superior to all other peoples in their call as God's servant race. Only these descendants of the 12 tribes of Israel scattered abroad have carried God's Word, the Bible, throughout the world, have used His Laws in the establishment of their civil governments and are the "Christians" opposed by the Satanic Anti-Christ forces of this world who do not recognize the true and living God.[12]

And this understanding of themselves as God's chosen people destined for blessing and foreordained to rule God's nation requires that "true" white Christians battle the evil forces in their midst. In this case, Identity devotes particular attention to locating evil among Jewish people, whom they see as the literal embodiment of evil. The doctrinal statement continues, "WE BELIEVE in an existing being known as the Devil or Satan and called the Serpent, who has a literal "seed" or posterity in the earth commonly called Jews today. These children of Satan through Cain who have throughout history always been a curse to true Israel, the Children of God, because of a natural enmity between the two races, because they do the works of their father the Devil and because they please not God, and are contrary to all men, though they often pose as ministers of righteousness. The ultimate end of this evil race whose hands bear the blood of our Savior and all the righteous slain upon the earth, is Divine judgment."[13] Although Christian Identity theology is, perhaps, the most extreme example of contemporary American constructions of evil that rely on racializing—and Identity's perception of Jewishness is certainly just as racialized as is its understanding of blackness—the persistence of racism and anti-Semitism requires that we place these groups on a spectrum in which far too many people hold to some, albeit tempered, version of these beliefs.

The location of evil in racial difference has not remained the exclusive province of white Americans, nor has the identification between race and divinely ordained destiny. Throughout the late nineteenth century, many black Christians made use of the biblical story of the sons of Noah to map a destiny for African Americans that also attempted to explain how God could have allowed them to be enslaved. James Theodore Holly, the Protestant Episcopal Bishop of Haiti, explored these issues in his 1884 essay, "The Divine Plan of Human Redemption in its Ethnological Development." Holly sets aside the oft-told story of Ham's sin and the curse on Canaan as the justification for the enslavement of people of African descent and, instead, turns to a discussion of the importance of "the tribal divisions of the human race" in the carrying out of God's plan.[14] In this version, the sons of Ham are not cursed, but are those chosen to effect the final stage of God's program for human redemption without whom it cannot be completed. Slavery, for Holly, served the purpose of exposing African Americans to Christianity so that they could become the exemplars of true Christianity:

The African race has been a servant of servants to their
brethren of the other races during all the long and
dreary ages of the Hebrew and Christian [European]
dispensations. And it is this service that they have so
patiently rendered through blood and tears that shall finally obtain for them the noblest of places of service in
the Coming Kingdom. Thus, what has been a curse to
them under Gentile tyranny will become a blessing to
them under the mild and beneficent reign of Christ."[15]

While late nineteenth century thinkers in this mode mediated on African American difference from whites as evidence of a destiny of significance, a number of twentieth
century African American figures have adopted an approach similar to that of Christian Identity; in this case,
however, they have located evil in whiteness. The Lost-
Found Nation of Islam is perhaps the best-known group to
take up this theological position. Nation of Islam cosmology narrates the creation of races, with black people as the
original people and whites, a race weak and "more suscep-
tible to wickedness and evil,"[16] coming into existence
through the machinations of Yacub, a scientist bent on
causing trouble. Thus, in Nation of Islam theology, whites
are quite literally evil. Similarly, the members of the House
of David insist on locating evil in racial difference. The
group's members believe themselves to be the descendants
of the twelve Tribes of Israel, and include among the Israelites people of African descent as well as various Native
Americans in North, Central, and South America. In their
theology, whites are the descendants of Esau and are
understood to be "the vessels of wrath created for destruction."[17] The Israeli Church of Universal Practical Knowledge, a group with beliefs similar to those of the House of
David, has begun to focus particularly on the year 2000

and the coming of God's judgment in what it calls "the final showdown between the Most High and Christ vs. Satan
[Esau]."[18] In these instances, rather than challenge the
equation of difference and evil upon which constructions
of race are predicated, these groups merely invert the hierarchy, placing themselves on top and whites on the bottom.

It is impossible to convey how deeply destructive the persistent location of evil in blackness has been to African
American communities and individuals. I consider the
drive to shuffle hierarchies in order to attempt to exercise
power over others (as evidenced in the Nation of Islam, for
example) to be one manifestation of this destructive construction of evil. James Baldwin spoke about the psychological damage of this social construction of evil in an open
letter to Angela Davis in 1970, just after she had been imprisoned. He wrote, "The American triumph—in which
the American tragedy has always been implicit—was to
make Black people despise themselves. When I was little I
despised myself, I did not know any better. And this
meant, albeit unconsciously, or against my will, or in great
pain, that I also despised my father. *And* my mother. *And*
my brothers. *And* my sisters. . . . Everything supported
this sense of reality, nothing denied it. . . . So one was
ready, when human terrors came, to bow before a white
God who was unable to raise a finger to do so little as to
help you pay your rent, unable to be awakened in time to
help you save your child."[19] W. E. B. Du Bois posed the
question to himself in his 1903 text, *The Souls of Black
Folk*: "How does it feel to be a problem?" Perhaps a more
apt question might be: "How does it feel to be constructed
as evil?" But blackness and Jewishness are not the only significant locations of imaginings about evil in America and

we must be attentive to the damage being done in a number of other communities in contemporary America.

In our America at the end of the twentieth century, we have seen the emergence of yet another tremendously powerful construction of evil in the world, a construction that has become an American obsession. Not surprisingly, Christian Identity theologians have articulated this construction in the most straightforward and clear-cut manner, declaring that "Homosexuality is an abomination before God and should be punished by death."[20] It would not be an exaggeration to say that a wide range of Americans—religious or not—locate the evil of the present moment among lesbians and gay men. Without question, however, religious individuals and institutions have been at the forefront of the movements that demonize sexual minorities. The Southern Baptist Convention has made the curtailment of human rights for lesbian and gay Americans a central part of its agenda, as has James Dobson's Focus on the Family, the Union of Orthodox Rabbis of the United States and Canada, and legions of other groups.

Perhaps the most noteworthy aspect of the recent demonization of gay and lesbian Americans is the insistence of people like James Dobson and the football player Reggie White on seeing racism as evil and at the same time promoting the view of homosexuality as sin. Significantly, many African American Christians have participated in this discourse quite vigorously. In a March 1998 speech before the Wisconsin Legislature, Reggie White advanced the notion that America is a Christian patriarchy in which some deserve rights and others do not:

> we've allowed this sin [homosexuality] to run rampant in our nation and because it has run rampant in our nation, our nation is in the condition it is today. Sometimes

when people talk about this sin, they've been accused of being racist. I'm offended that homosexuals will say that homosexuals deserve rights. Any man in America deserves rights, but homosexuals are trying to compare their plight with the plight of black men or black people. In the process of history, homosexuals have never been castrated, millions of them never died. Homosexuality is a decision, it's not a race. People from all different ethnic backgrounds live in this lifestyle. But people from all different ethnic backgrounds also are liars and cheaters and malicious and back-stabbing.[21]

The argument, then, that the socially constructed categories of race and sexuality are natural, rigid, and divinely ordained requires groups like the Southern Baptist Convention to argue that any attempt to prevent discrimination against lesbians and gay men is tantamount to providing unfair "advantage." Thus, in a 1998 resolution adopted to condemn President Clinton's signing of "Executive Order 11478, Equal Employment Opportunity in the Federal Government,"[22] the Southern Baptist Convention asserted that "homosexual politics is masquerading as 'civil rights,' in order to exploit the moral high ground of the civil rights movement even though homosexual conduct and other learned sexual deviance have nothing in common with the moral movement to stop discrimination against race and gender." And it resolved to "oppose all efforts to provide government endorsements, sanction, recognition, acceptance or civil rights advantage on the basis of homosexuality."[23]

It seems clear to me that, just as the production of ideas about race makes possible and maintains domination on the part of whites who invest themselves in racial hierarchy, so too ideas about sexuality serve to make those not in the minority feel justified in oppressing those who are. The

current discourse that demonizes sexual minorities reveals
a dogged unwillingness to recognize that the categories of
identity that help to shape who we are socially constructed.
Hysteria about homosexuality points to a failure of the
imagination to see that these categories emerge in relation
to power and that to accept them as "natural" embeds in
them evaluations of good vs. evil. Not only does this construction of difference as evil divide people, it authorizes
violence and domination that far too many people accept
as justified. And, sadly, we have at least as long a journey
with regard to dismantling homophobia as we have had
with racism, sexism, and anti-Semitism, struggles all still
ongoing.

Anna Deavere Smith's performance piece *Fires in the Mirror: Crown Heights, Brooklyn and Other Identities*[24] is perhaps the most powerful, if not the most heartening, attempt to chip away at the unwillingness to extend beyond
the individual view. In this stunning piece of work, Smith
embodies various people she interviewed over a period of
years on themes that arose out of the conflict between the
Caribbean immigrant and the Hasidic communities of
Crown Heights. The conflict that had been brewing for
years erupted in the aftermath of the death of Gavin Cato,
the young son of Caribbean immigrants who was struck by
a car driven by a Hasidic man in August 1991. In the chaos
that followed Cato's death, Yankel Rosenbaum, an Austra-
lian rabbinical student, was murdered by a group of black
men. Smith's piece presents multiple perspectives on these
events, turning them around and around and refusing to
"take sides." In this insistence on constantly turning away
from easy answers, Smith forces her viewers to analyze

their own perspectives as constructed in relation to race, gender, religion, national origin, and a host of other elements of individual and community identity. Her work is so effective in this regard precisely because the interviews and voices of the people take place in the context of an event that has ruptured human connections and sent people into the safety of bunkered communities. Truly, she has taken on a difficult task.

In interviewing famous players in the story, central figures whom circumstance propelled into the spotlight, and anonymous residents of the neighborhood, Smith sought to explore the contours of "American character in the way that people speak."[25] And, indeed, Smith brings out the profound poetry and power in the thought and speech of people, many of whom she encountered on the streets of Crown Heights. But most compelling about Smith's work is her attempt to make a meaningful social experience from the humble act of repeating someone else's words, allowing them to speak for themselves. She writes about the process by which she arrived at her approach to performance: "I needed evidence that you could find a character's psychological reality by 'inhabiting' that character's words. . . . If we were to inhabit the speech pattern of another, and walk in the speech of another, we could find the individuality of the other and experience that individuality viscerally."[26] And in this sometimes jarring performance of repeating the words of others—of Smith, a black woman "becoming" various black and white men, white women, young people and old—she provides a way for the audience to become more attentive to the people whose words she conveys. I find it significant that, while Smith arrived at this performance approach in part through her search for an acting technique, she insists that it also provides a model for social interactions outside the theater: "The spirit of acting is the *travel* from the self to the other. This 'self-based' method seemed to come to a spiritual halt. It saw the self as the ultimate home of the character. To me, the search for character is constantly in motion. It is the quest that moves back and forth between the self and the other."[27] Thus, in the world of Smith's performance, her audience learns how to listen, how to attempt to view and understand an experience or event from multiple perspectives. In providing these lessons, she provides tools for social interaction outside the theater and beyond the particular event that gave rise to her performance.

James Baldwin came to a similar conclusion concerning the potential of human interactions for moving the individual beyond the limited boundaries of the self: "If I write you a letter, for example, I am trying to tell you something or ask you something—whatever the message, it can be, finally, only myself, hoping to be delivered. If I speak to you, I want you to hear me—to hear *me*—and to see me. Speech and language, however ceremonious, complex, and convoluted, are a way of revealing one's nakedness; and this revelation is, really, our only human hope. But this hope is strangled if one, or both of us, is lying."[28] For me, the most profound sort of lie rests in the constructions of evil in American history—but certainly not limited to America by any means—that have vilified people on the basis of skin color, sex, sexuality, religion, class. This kind of lie authorizes separation, neglect, and violence and can never enable the kinds of human connections for which someone like Anna Deavere Smith reaches in her work and which should guide us all. Angela Davis put it well in her inter-

view with Smith for *Fires in the Mirror*: "I'm not suggesting that we do not anchor ourselves in our communities; I
feel very anchored in my various communities. But I think
that, to use a metaphor, the rope attached to that anchor
should be long enough to allow us to move into other communities, to understand and learn. I've been thinking a lot
about the need to make more intimate these connections
and associations and to really take on the responsibility of
learning."[29]

THE POLITICS OF CONVERSION
AND THE CIVILIZATION OF FRIDAY

Walter E. Fluker

At last he lays his head flat upon the ground, close to my
foot, and sets my other foot upon his head, as he has done
before, and after this made all signs to me of subjection,
servitude, and submission imaginable, to let me know
how he would serve me as long as he lived. I understood
him in many things, and let him know I was very well
pleased with him. In a little time I began to speak to him,
and teach him to speak to me; and, first, I made him know
his name should be called Friday, which was the day I
saved his life. I likewise taught him to say master, and
then let him know that was to be my name. [Robinson
Crusoe regarding his man, Friday.][1]

AFRICAN AMERICAN LEADERSHIP
IN A NEW KEY

W ITH a renaissance in scholarship on Malcolm X
(El-Hajj Malik El-Shabazz) and Martin Luther
King, Jr., conversations within and beyond the African
American community have focused on the political and social strategies of these two men as resources in articulating
a new vision for the struggle against the jagged and complex congeries of race, gender, and class, and their impact
on plight of African Americans. Sorely neglected in these
conversations is the place of spirituality in the social and
political thought and praxis of these two men. Beyond
their respective approaches to the political and economic
spheres of Black existence is a more profound and relevant

legacy. Malcolm and Martin leave living testaments of their hope: an irrepressible hope that will not relinquish its hold on the redemptive possibilities inherent in human beings.

Their search for personal wholeness and transformation brought them to the forefront of a political movement that changed the direction of the nation and the world. But the crass and critical issues of our day demand that a "new breed of cat" come on the scene, who, like Malcolm and Martin, are bold and courageous enough to journey through the valley of tradition and orthodoxy. Men and women who are able to wage battle with the legions of doubts and fears that stand guard over our entry into a future laden with ambiguity. The lives of Malcolm and Martin, and the dangerous memories they leave, are summons for a new vanguard of visionaries: a generation of new leaders who are spiritually disciplined and intellectually astute, able to interpret the present madness that is upon us, and to prescribe new formulae and possibilities for a people rapidly losing hope.

Martin and Malcolm represent "dangerous memories" and redemptive possibilities in the struggle for justice. In Malcolm and Martin, spirituality and social transformation are the dominant themes which define and make available the resources for this hope. For King, this theme is the basis for his articulation of the beloved community ideal. For Malcolm, spirituality and social transformation are the keys which decipher the sphinxlike riddle of his ironic quest for just relations among human beings.

Make no mistake, Malcolm and Martin were different. Attempts to create complementarity between the two where it does not exist are unproductive and futile. But while there are distinct differences in approaches to their respective goals, beyond (perhaps, beneath) their differences in methodology and ideology lies the common quest for personal wholeness and identity in a recalcitrant, racist society that militates against such possibility. The work of social transformation in both men is inextricably bound with their religious quests for authentic personhood. Their personal quests ultimately involve searches for radical change in public policy and practice. One can hardly miss this truth in reviewing the spiritual developments of these Black titans.[2]

Cornel West has brilliantly analyzed the contemporary moral straitjacket which has stymied the potential for creative national leadership and wreaked deleterious effects on African American leadership in particular. He cites the foibles of structuralist and behaviorist interpretations and recommendations for those at the bottom of the American social ladder. He argues that this debate "conceals the most basic issue now facing black America: *the nihilistic threat to its very existence.*" Beyond political and economic remedies, while significant, the threat of personal meaningless, despair, and worthlessness, brought about in large part by unbridled market forces and political chicanery, is the real challenge that confronts African Americans and the national community. West calls for a new kind of moral leadership which moves beyond the "pitfalls of racial reasoning" and the lack of courage to address "*the market moralities of black life*" and "*the crisis of black leadership.*" He recommends "*a politics of conversion*" fueled by a love ethic which has historically sustained the African American community. Important for our purposes is his identification of memory and hope as key resources in the politics of conversion: "Self-love and love of others," he writes, "are both modes toward increasing self-valuation and encouraging political resistance in one's community. These modes of valuation and resistance are rooted in *subversive memory*—the best of one's past without romantic nostalgia—and guided by a universal ethic of love."[3]

West's call for a new kind of moral leadership emanating from the grassroots is not a new phenomenon in American society, but what is refreshing and potentially creative is his sensitivity to the interrelated necessities of personal and social transformation. A significant element of this new kind of leadership is the emphasis on transformation which requires a return to memory as a basis for hope without romanticization and trivilization of the arduous paths which must be trod in order to translate this memory into praxis. In this respect the dangerous memories of Martin and Malcolm are important, but not adequate in and of themselves to fuel the assault against hopelessness that plagues our beleaguered communities. While the dream of the beloved community of Martin Luther King, Jr., still inspires us to uplift the dignity and worth of human personality, even toward our enemies, his method of nonviolent direct action may not be adequate to transform the hardened and intransigent structures of a morally reprobate society. And likewise, while the rugged vision of African American unity, articulated by Malcolm X, still reminds us that self-love and militancy are the logical demands for powerless and oppressed peoples, still they do not answer the ultimate need for a relational love ethic in a universe that cannot exist without it. What we need is not an either/ or alternative between Malcolm and Martin, or between militant aggression or moral suasion. We need rather a new creative vision which is a synthesis of both.

The scope and shape of this new vision will depend

largely on our willingness as individuals and as a nation to enter the no-trespassing zones of this world system and to inquire about the meaning of our existence on these shores. More fundamentally, it will demand an internal revolution, in King's language, of values and priorities. In order to make this journey into the interior we need guides who have left maps of the spiritual landscape. It will require most of all, a radical conversion of our social understandings of self, which are the products of a competitive market economy that pits individuals and racial/ethnic groups against one another. For African Americans, in particular, it means literally a return to memory, a soul journey in the caves of our ancestors where we hear again the rhythmic murmurings of the Black and angry dead—but more so, where again we learn the lessons of those who surround us as a great cloud of witnesses.[4]

THE CIVILIZATION OF FRIDAY

Cornel West's call for a *politics of conversion* presupposes the nexus of memory and hope. African American leadership cannot begin this spiritual process until there is a willingness to return to its religio-cultural roots of sacrifice and service. This return to a sane place will require a radical deconstruction of self in the midst of a multiplicity of forces that stand guard over our entry into a new future. In other words, the politics of conversion presupposes psychic conversion. The psychic conversion of Malcolm and the transformed nonconformity which King talked about involve a type of existential death—a blessed irrationality born of the refusal to submit to market mentalities and cultural cages which inhibit the birthing of new names and redemptive possibilities.

The anatomy of the kind of personal transformation which is an integral dimension of the politics of conversion can be seen in the dynamics of the master/slave relation imbedded in the dominant discourse of Euro-western hegemonic practices. The civilization of Friday, Robinson Crusoe's man, offers some insight into the modalities of self-devaluation and the need to move beyond the superimposed categories of domination and subordination in search of authentic selfhood. It is at once a window through which we can see the underlying dynamics of slave morality and the internalized gaze which inhibits conversation between the builders of the American tower of Babel and the stones that the builders rejected.

The name given to the "savage" whom Crusoe rescued on the deserted island, where he had been shipwrecked twenty-three years earlier, is of particular importance. He named him "Friday"—the day of the week he "saved his life." The ascription "Friday" denotes the day of the week in which the savage is brought into "real time," that is, civilized time—the time of the master. Crusoe not only names him, but in effect names his world, his etiquette, his language, his symbols, his culture—indeed his humanity. In Crusoe's mind, before meeting him, the child/savage was in bondage to the elemental forces of nature. His existence is bestial, but the master teaches him his language. Even more is at stake in Friday's civilization. For Crusoe, it is the religion of Providence that legitimizes his function as master and teacher. Race, religion, and culture meld together in a seamless construction of hierarchy. In order for Friday to be saved he must become civilized. Friday understands his role and consciously subjects himself to his master.

"At last he lays his head flat upon the ground, close to my foot, and sets my other foot upon his head, as he has done before, and after this made all signs to me of subjection, servitude, and submission imaginable, to let me know how he would serve me as long as he lived." Friday has learned through the appropriation of the master's language that his place in the hierarchy of the cosmos is at his master's feet. Incivility is sin, licentiousness, bestiality, mindlessness, chaos, and all manner of evil.

Better not get too loud, Friday! Don't touch holy things, Friday! Be still, Friday! Refuse to be a body! Friday, you have neither voice nor eyes. Be *good,* Friday.[5]

This particular sample of Western literary discourse provides a helpful entree into the struggle of African Americans to achieve and conform to an image of self which is not catacombed in the mindless mazes of subjection to an ethic which predisposes them to a life of inferiority and second-class citizenship. But the challenge of African Americans to free themselves from the gaze of Crusoe is double-edged. One cannot begin this conversation in a vacuum. Friday cannot be free until he rebels against Crusoe. Crusoe's identity, on the other hand, is bound to his perception of Friday. Friday's rebellion creates a kind of cultural apoplexy in which Crusoe is both victimizer and patient, because Crusoe—not Friday—is the object of rebellion. Yet there is an even more nefarious warfare raging within Friday. How can he destroy the master without initiating his own demise?

America stands in the place of Crusoe, the civilizer and the patient. Friday is the destroyer and the redeemer. Friday's freedom is an exercise in death. He must die in order to live, he must rebel in order to hope. When Friday announces his intention, Crusoe tightens the noose, but in tightening the noose he destroys himself.

Who *frees* Friday from himself? God, religion, politics, economic development, and all the recommendations that shout at him daily from a fragmented discourse which falls back on itself?[6] No, Friday must free himself from Crusoe's gaze. This internalized look of the other, this stalking fear of madness. Friday must discover his name as a counter-name to the ascription which Crusoe has given— but even more, Friday must find a new name, a name not proscribed and prescribed by the master's time. Friday's rebellion is against his socially constructed self—he must for the first time see himself through his own eyes and speak with his own voice. This requires a journey into the "cave"—that trysting place where he wrestles with the shadows, the appearances that flash against wall of his consciousness—a consciousness shaped by years of bondage to the name, the thing outside of himself. It is at once recognition, defiance, and play: recognition of the twisted and contorted stare at one's self; insight into the incivility of the Cross which is a personal act of transgression and defiant speech; and linguistic play on a morality which signifies on all *good* Fridays.

A STRANGE FREEDOM

It is a strange freedom to be adrift in the world of men,
to act with no accounting, to go nameless up and down
the streets of other minds where no salutation greets
and no sign is given to mark the place one calls one's
own. . . . The name marks the claim a man stakes against
the world; it is the private banner under which he moves
which is his right whatever else betides. The name is a
man's water mark above which the tide can never rise.
It is the thing he holds that keeps him in the way when
every light has failed and every marker has been destroyed. It is the rallying point around which a man
gathers all that he means by himself. It is his announce-
ment to life that he is present and accounted for in all his

parts. To be made anonymous and to give the acquiescence of the heart is to live without life, and for such a
one, even death is no dying.

To be known, to be called by one's name, is to find
one's place and hold it against the hordes of hell. This is
to *know* one's value for one's self alone. It is to honor an
act as one's very own, it is to live a life that is one's very
own, it is to worship a God who is one's very own.[7]

Howard Thurman's work is an excellent place to begin
this initial task of conversion, the transformation of subjugated consciousness. He often stated, "The time and place
of a person's life on earth is the time and place of the body,
but the meaning and significance of that life is as far-
reaching and redemptive as the gifts, the dedication, the
response to the demand of the times, the total commitment
of one's powers can make it."[8] What does it mean to *live* life
seriously (not to *take* life seriously)? To live freely and un-
encumbered by the necessity of always conforming to external things that limit our potential to be authentically
human in the world? Thurman thought it demanded a
journey into the interior, into those places we have sealed
off and secured with no-trespassing signs. It meant, for
him, an inward journey into dangerous territory, where the
real issues of life and death must be confronted, where the
"Angel with the flaming sword" greets us—where we are
not allowed entry unless we yield "the fluid center of our
consent."

> There is in every person an inward sea, and in that sea
> there is an island and on that island there is an altar and
> standing guard before that altar is the "angel with the
> flaming sword." Nothing can get by that angel to be
> placed upon that altar unless it has the mark of inner
> authority. Nothing passes "the angel with the flaming
> sword" to be placed upon your altar unless it be a part of
> "the fluid area of your consent." This is your link with
> the Eternal.[9]

This journey into the interior, according to Thurman, is not extraordinary; in many respects, it is far removed from what we normally call "religion." The Angel with the flaming sword is encountered in the mundane, earthly experiences of being and living in the world. At any junction in the road there may suddenly appear a sign, a flash, a burning bush, which places us in candidacy for this experience. Often in struggle, in crisis, in the heart of suffering and trial, one encounters the Angel, the truth about one's self, the mendacious stereotypes about self and others, and the subtle and surreptious ways in which one has been named.

Luther Smith correctly observes that for Thurman "the crucible of relationship" provides the hermeneutical key for ascertaining meaning in the various modes of existence in which one finds oneself. In this perspective, epistemological and axiological questions are grounded in a moral anthropology that avoids the dichotomous portrayal of the self as an irreconcilable tension between nature and spirit. Rather, for Thurman, the self is essentially relational and agential. Ratiocination is a secondary act. "The deed reveals meaning. Meaning does not exist as a disembodied force, but it becomes evident through relationships." All meaningful knowledge is for the sake of action, and all meaningful action is for the sake of loving relationship. Religious faith, therefore, is not to be confused with dogmatic assertions fixed in creed and formal statements. Rather it has to do with "literal truth and the conviction it inspires." This truth is disclosed in creative encounter with a "Thou" in lived-community with others.[10]

Thurman emphasized the dynamic, intuitive nature of truth. He characterized intuitive knowledge as "immediate, direct, and not an inference from logic. . . . It is an awareness of literal truth directly perceived." In Thurman's conceptualization of spirituality and social transformation, which he referred to as "the inner life and world-mindedness," the individual is the point of departure. A persistent note in his thinking is that one must begin with oneself, with one's own "working paper." The development of a sense of self is the basis upon which one comes to understand one's own unique potential and self-worth. Without a sense of self, the person drifts aimlessly through life without a true understanding of his or her place in existence. A healthy sense of self is garnered out of a dynamic tension between the individual's self-fact and self-image.

The person's self-fact is her or his inherent worth as a child of God. It is the central fact that one is part of the very movement of life itself. The individual's self-image is formed by relationships with others, and to a large extent, self-image determines one's destiny. However, the individual's case must ultimately rest with his or her self-fact of intrinsic worth. Thurman writes, "The responsibility for living with meaning and dignity can never be taken away from the individual." This is a significant point for his treatment of the individual's response to dehumanizing onslaughts like racism and other forces that work against human potential and community.[11] Consequently, his usage of terms like "inner life" or "inner awareness" refer to more than the formal discursive activity of the mind, but rather include the entire range of the individual's self-awareness.[12] "Inner life" means

> . . . the awareness of the individual's responsiveness to
> realities that are transcendent in character, emanating
> from a core of Reality of which the individual is aware

and of which the individual is also aware that he is a
part. The inner life, therefore, is activity that takes place
within consciousness, but does not originate there and is
a part of a Reality central to all life and is at once the
ground of all awareness. It is there that man becomes
conscious of his meaning and destiny as a child, an off-
spring of God.[13]

The "interiority of religious experience," as I am using
it, is synonymous with Thurman's terminology "the inner
life." "Interiority" means to belong to the inner constitution or concealed nature of something; it connotes dimen-
sionality, that which lies away from the border or shore. For
Thurman, therefore, religious experience is a journey into
the inner regions of self, an exploration into that which is
normally concealed from the conscious mind. It is in this
experience of self-exploration that one discovers what she
or he amounts to, one's inherent value and worth as a child
of God.[14]

Since the cultivation of the inner life is the basis for the
development of a genuine sense of self and authentic existence in the world, it is in this process that one discovers
one's name and destiny as a child of God. Thurman is
acutely aware of the danger of subjectivism and the privat-
ization of meaning implied in the emphasis on the development of inner consciousness. He guards against this tendency by accentuating the need for empirical verification
of what one experiences in her or his inner life. "The real
questions at issue here," he contends, "are, how may a man
know he is not being deceived? Is there any way by which
he may know beyond doubt, and therefore with verification, that what he experiences is authentic and genuine?"[15]
Religious faith, therefore, is "the tutor" or the "unseen
model" by which one structures the facts of his or her experience. For this reason, Thurman counseled:

[T]he person concerned about social change must not
only understand the materials with which he has to do,
the things which he is trying to manipulate, to reorder,
to refashion, but again and again he must expose the
roots of his mind to the literal truth that is the tutor of
the facts, the orderer and reorderer of the facts of his
experience.[16]

This must be done, Thurman contended, so that in the
quest for social justice, one's vision of society never con-
forms to some external pattern, but is "modeled and
shaped in accordance to the innermost transformation that
is going on in his spirit."[17] Accordingly, it was his insistence that those who were engaged in acts of liberation
continually examine the sources of their motivation and
the ways in which the circling series of social processes
which they seek to change are related to their spiritual pilgrimage. Always, the primary questions for the social activ-
ist are, "*What are you trying to do with your life? What kind
of person are you trying to become?*"[18]

It was Thurman's conviction that the individual in his
or her actions "is trying to snare into the body of his facts,
his conviction of those facts." He cautioned, however, that
faith thusly understood always runs the risk of becoming
idolatrous, as in patriotic visions of "the American way."[19]
Consequently, one must always examine the motivational
content of action that involves a tutoring of the will by the
unseen model that, for Thurman, was the truth which is
resident within the individual. Here the issues of *identity*,
purpose, and *method* are combined in relation to the social
context in which the individual finds himself or herself.

For the marginalized person, this exploration into interiority is especially significant since it underscores the pre-
eminence of self-actualization in the midst of recalcitrant

and obtrusive power arrangements that war against personal meaning and social space. According to Thurman, there is within each individual a basic need to be cared for and understood in a relationship with another at a point that is beyond all that is good and evil. In religious experience, this inner necessity for love is fulfilled in encounter with God and in community with others. In the presence of God and in relation with others, the person is affirmed and becomes aware of being dealt with totally.

> Whether he is a good person or a bad person, he is being
> dealt with at a point beyond all that is limiting, and all
> that is creative within him. He is dealt with at the core of
> his being, and at that core he is touched and released.[20]

As one dares to ask the primary questions of identity, purpose, and method, and is willing to be tutored by the "sound of the genuine" that is within,[21] a refreshing occurs; a new sense of self and Presence emerges which enables one to reenter the struggle with new courage and determination. Thurman understood this quest for personal space to involve defiant activity, for it presupposes that the one's liberative quest in society cannot ultimately be divorced from one's wrestling with the internal issues of power and dominance.[22] Jesus, like the rest of humanity, was not immune from the dilemmas of existence and the temptations to personally dominate others and to cling to security and comfort. Jesus' defiance is best articulated in his conscious choice to go to Jerusalem though he knew it meant death to challenge an obdurate culture.[23]

Ultimately, the interiority of religious experience brings us to crossroads where we must "choose."[24] Thurman believed that this is the faith that is courage and the courage that is faith. No one escapes this awful demand, especially no one who dares to challenge the political and economic structures which name one's position in the world. The challenge before the leadership in African American communities, and indeed the leadership of the nation, is one that calls forth this daring to enter the unsafe places of the transformed nonconformists. This daring to speak to the world out of the depths of a new-found, twice-born courage. It is an encounter with the Crucified One, that dangerous memory from the past and the redemptive possibility of the present. It is for this reason that black theological discourse must explore more intensely the relationship of spirituality and social transformation and the nexus of memory and hope in the liberation of Friday.

PREACHING
& SCRIPTURE

Linking Texts with Contexts

The Biblical Sermon as Social Commentary

Carolyn Ann Knight

And seek the peace of the City, where I have caused you to be carried away captive, and pray to the Lord for it; for in its peace you will have peace.

—JEREMIAH 29:7 (NEW KING JAMES VERSION)

A S THE Christian church braces itself for the arrival of the twenty-first century, there is good news and bad news. The good news is this: there is a renewed interest in the church and in preaching. The bad news is this: the demand for relevant, needs-meeting, issue-addressing preaching has never been greater. In a world like this, people are returning to the church with a sense of expectancy that the men and women who have emerged from the community of faith and taken a place in the pulpit do in fact have a word from the Lord that will speak specifically to the needs and issues of society in their generation. Many and varied are the social issues that confront the elderly, men and women, the baby boomers and busters, generation X, gays and lesbians, the disabled and physically challenged, and youth and children. Is there a word from the Lord? Is there no balm in Gilead? I believe that there is. The word from the Lord and the balm in Gilead can be found in biblical sermons that are targeted toward social issues.

Many years ago I read this statement: "When there is a strong pulpit, there is a strong society." Even though the name of the person who made this statement has escaped my memory, it still affects the very high view that I hold of preaching. I am greatly encouraged by the revival of biblical preaching that is sweeping this country. *Time* magazine and others have documented in cover stories the return of the "baby-boomer" generation to houses of worship in this land. They are returning to churches and synagogues expecting to hear something from the rabbi, minister, or priest that will speak specifically and concretely to their circumstances. They want to know what God is doing in their world and how they should respond.

There is a great need now for men and women who preach to deliver relevant sermons from their pulpits. It is the responsibility of seminaries and Bible colleges to see that their students are equipped and prepared to preach such sermons. This brief essay sets out to discuss the nature of the biblical sermon as social commentary. Initially, I set out to develop a homiletical method, an approach to developing and designing sermons that deal with contemporary social issues. Looking critically at the world of the Bible, I believe that the African American sermon serves as a paradigm for this type of preaching. I began with the firm belief that sermons, in addition to providing a way of salvation, wholeness, and a personal relationship with Jesus Christ, must hold some social significance if they are to be relevant to the listener. I have always believed that preaching is essentially a redemptive activity. In the very act of preaching, God encounters, probes, and challenges the human spirit. But preaching is also a transformative activity. God uses preaching as an avenue through which lives, and thereby the world, can be changed for the better.

Preaching is also a theological act, an activity that involves God in the day-to-day affairs of humanity and links Christianity to the concrete. Ronald J. Sider and Michael A. King, in *Preaching about Life in a Threatening World*, demonstrate the theological dimension of preaching. We are reminded that "salvation is not just a spiritual or other-worldly reality. It has radical implications for this real and desperate world, a world in which the poor and hungry and tortured need more than salvation from their personal sin, though they need that too."[1] Christine M. Smith, in *Preaching as Weeping, Confessing and Resistance*, also makes the case for preaching as a theological act:

> A vital preaching ministry includes the skills of the so-phisticated communicator, the attentiveness of the biblical exegete, the social analyses of the most discerning sociologist, but first and foremost it is the craft and act of a working theologian. It is a theological act because preachers are called to reflect upon, and struggle with, ultimate religious questions in life.[2]

Smith presses her claim when she says, "Preaching is an act of public theological naming. It is an act of disclosing and articulating the truths about our present human existence."[3]

PROJECT NEEDS ASSESSMENT

Karl Barth, that great theologian of the twentieth century, is often quoted as saying that "every preacher should prepare sermons with the Bible in one hand and the newspaper in the other." I am sure that if Professor Barth were alive in the high-tech environment of the 1990s, he would suggest that Cable News Network (CNN) and "Headline News" be included in every preacher's study. This suggestion would not be hard to receive because we live an age where the rapidly changing scenario of our nation and the world make it necessary for the preacher to have almost instantaneous information at his or her disposal. Preachers like everyone else, are bombarded with ongoing updates of current events. As they sit in their study awaiting the Holy Spirit, the world changes before their eyes. On any given day, issues of global war, homelessness, violence, homophobia, women's rights, HIV and AIDS flash across the television screen. They are impossible to ignore as we prepare for Sunday's sermon.

With the understanding that God is actively involved in the events of the world, and the conviction that the Word of God gives us a mandate for appropriate response to such events, I wanted to teach a graduate-level preaching course during my time at Union Seminary and Interdenominational Theological Center that would enable seminarians and experienced practitioners to design, develop, and deliver sermons dealing with contemporary social issues. I also wanted to help preachers see the need to link ancient biblical texts with these issues so that the hearers of their sermons would have a clear understanding of what God is saying and doing in the world and their active response in the world would be consistent with the claims of God as found in the Scriptures. In order to do this, a methodology was needed to reach what Thomas H. Troeger calls, "the landscape of the heart."

In *Preaching as a Social Act*, Troeger says the problem with most preaching is that "sermons sound like nothing more than another editorial, worthy perhaps of a responsible citizen's reflection, but never sending lightning and thunder over the landscape of the heart."[4] Troeger makes the following suggestion for preaching on social issues: "In the face of such a profound spiritual crisis, the task of homiletics is to revitalize the religious imagination so that it creates a sense of open space in front of people, thereby giving them enough hope to work for social change."[5]

Preaching makes sense as listeners come to know and understand God's involvement in light of their existential reality. It is one thing for people to hear sermons that address grand themes of faith, hope, and love. It is quite another to hear those same themes addressed in the light of an HIV/AIDS epidemic and against the backdrop of racism, sexism, and economic recession. What is God saying about the issues that face a people on the brink of the twenty-first century? How is the preacher to give an impartial, objective exegesis of biblical texts that will help listeners understand God's action in the world? Samuel D. Proctor, writing in *Preaching about Crisis in the Community*, provides an answer:

> The preacher has the unique responsibility to stand tall in the midst of our moral confusion, our spiritual estrangement, and our lost opportunities and to declare that God is with us in our situation. News commentators, columnists, analysts, and television anchor people may make plain what our condition is, with meticulous detail and fastidious accuracy, but no one except the preacher is expected to proclaim that above, around, beneath and throughout this deep, dark morass lies the pervasive purpose of a loving and caring God.[6]

What do the ancient texts of the Bible have to say to a world poised on the brink of the twenty-first century? Is it possible to link the world of the Bible to our contemporary world? If so, who is responsible for making the connection and how? All these questions are essential to a discussion about preaching on social issues. The answers, although simple, do not readily supply the methodology for preaching on social issues. But the ancient texts of the Bible have much to say to our contemporary context, and the preacher is responsible for making that connection.

Preaching on social issues, bringing the world of the Bible into the world of contemporary Christians, is the most critical task of preaching today. People who are returning to church these days are doing so because they are in urgent need of a word beyond this world that speaks cogently, relevantly, and powerfully to their situation in this world. This is the preacher's task, to convince Christians in this time that the world of the Bible has a fresh word for them. These hearers want sermons that provide a way of salvation, of wholeness, and a personal relationship with Jesus Christ, but beyond that they want sermons that hold some significance for the world in which they live.

Preaching is essentially a redemptive activity. In the very act of preaching, God encounters, probes, and challenges the human spirit. Preaching is one of God's methods of saving the world: "For the message of the cross is foolishness to those who are perishing, but to us who are being saved it is the power of God. . . . For since, in the wisdom of God, the world through wisdom did not know God, it pleased God through the foolishness of the message preached to save those who believe" (1 Corinthians 1:18, 21 [New King James Version]). But preaching is also a transformative activity. God uses preaching as an avenue through which lives, and thereby the world, can be changed for the better.

To understand preaching as an avenue whereby the world is transformed is to understand preaching as an evangelistic activity. And there can be no true evangelism without preaching on social issues. Addressing these needs through the sermon is the preacher's way of announcing God's action in this world. In addressing social issues, the preacher brings the good news of God's solutions to critical social concerns. Our good news must be God's good news. Preaching on social issues must have as its bottom line God's solutions to the national and global concerns of our day.[7] It says to those listening that God is actively involved in the affairs of humankind. The sermon that addresses social issues uses the ancient texts of the Bible to say that God has acted in Israel and in Jesus, and God continues to act in the church today, transforming us and the world.

THE WORLD OF THE BIBLE

Preaching on social issues requires an understanding of the world of the Bible. To understand the world of the text and to interpret that text in a contemporary context is an act of faith that requires honest, identifiable engagement with the text. For Walter Brueggeman this is a "willful act of production of meaning,"[8] in which the community is at work with the text. The act of generating a text that can be heard by a contemporary listening community is an act of decisive faith, an act of construal and discernment on the part of the community of faith. The responsibility for bringing the community of faith to such a moment of decision is the preacher's:

> Interpretation is all the action between formation and reception that seeks to assert the authority and significance of the text. This interpretive step includes the classical creeds and commentaries, the long history of theological

reflection, contemporary scholarship, and contemporary church pronouncements. Above all, it includes the interpretative work of the preacher in the sermon.[9]

Brueggeman goes further:

> It is in the sermon that the church has done its decisive, faith-determining interpretation. The sermon is not an act of reporting on a test, but it is an act of making a new text visible and available. This new text in part is the old text, and in part is the imaginative construction of the preacher which did not exist until the moment of utterance by the preacher.[10]

It is the task of the homiletician and the preacher to interpret the function of the biblical in the life of the community.

> Often in homiletics there is a primary emphasis on the world of the text. Homileticians and preachers alike are concerned with such things as how sacred texts function in the life of the community, how texts are interpreted, how texts have evolved in meaning and interpretation in the life of the church, and how the literary and distinctive qualities of texts function in the liturgical and religious life of the people.[11]

How this function of interpretation is determined is an act of faith and imagination. It is an act of faith because it relies on the work of God's Spirit of truth. It is an act of the imagination because the interpreter and the listener have a part in determining the meaning of the text.

> The textual process is at every point an act of faith. In faithful interpretation, the entire process is governed by the work of God's Spirit of truth. It is this that permits interpretation to be an act of faith. The promise of faith is the conviction that in its formation, interpretation, and reception the text is a word of life that makes a difference. No part of this process is undertaken on the pretense that this is objective or neutral or a matter of indifference.[12]

The act of faith must be accompanied by imagination: "The transforming power of the church declines whenever it loses it religious imagination by which I mean its ability to envision and communicate images of an alternative reality that can break the sign of normative consciousness."[13]

Preaching on social issues requires an interpretation of the biblical text that will enable the community of faith to discern God's work in the act of personal and social transformation. This act of God can only be understand by the community through faith. Therefore, the personality of those who preach must be loving and winning, especially if preachers are to address social issues."[14] In addition,

> Anyone then, who is going to preach on social issues needs to understand the power of myth and its poetic language of image and symbol, their grip upon the language of the heart, and the enormous energies that they may release for good or evil. . . . Information and well-reasoned analysis belong in sermons, but they are ineffectual as long as the preacher has not entered the landscape of the heart and challenged the reigning metaphors of secularist national culture with images and narratives of faith.[15]

"Shoes That Fit Our Feet": The African-American Sermon Model

For the most part, preaching in the African American context responds to some critical societal need. Much preaching done in this context is evangelical in design in that it addresses a social need as a way of bringing individuals to personal salvation. Because of its history, rooted in one hundred and forty-four years of slavery, one hundred and twenty-five years of legalized segregation, countless years of second-class citizenship and degradation, and a resurgence of modern-day racism, African American preaching is a most appropriate paradigm for preaching on social issues.

The earliest exposure of African slaves to Christianity on these shores reveals that almost immediately the slaves noted contradictions in the sermons that they were hearing and in the God they had come to know in their heads, hearts, and spirits. "The preaching tradition of the Black ancestors did not spring into existence suddenly. It was developed during a long and often quite disconnected series of contacts between the Christian gospel, variously interpreted, and African men and women caught up in the Black experience of slavery and oppression."[16] Having been able to negotiate the contradictions, these Africans were to fashion their own "sermons" addressing the issues of their day.

Using what they knew of the prophets and what they understood about the power of God and the love of Jesus, they were able to convince their "listeners" that there was a better day coming. This was just the beginning. Because of the perilous predicament of the African American in America, the pulpit and the sermon became the major method of communication among a marginalized people. Because the pulpit was considered "free," the preacher was often considered the most independent person in the African American community. "The proclamation of the Black pulpit survives likewise because, in its isolation from the mainstream, it spoke and it speaks peculiarly to the needs of blacks."[17] The preacher could say things from the pulpit that no other professional of that era could say. The pulpit thus became more than just a place where the gospel and cute Bible stories could be heard: it became an agent for social change in the community.

From the pulpits of the African American church, rallies were planned, voters registered, marches organized, and monies raised. From those pulpits, listeners were sent out with their marching orders for conduct and decorum on the job and around "the man." From those pulpits, African American listeners learned what was "going down" and when. They did not make a noticeable distinction between the preachers' words and God's word: for the most part they were one. The preacher used the Bible to convince the listener that this is what God would have them to do and how God would have them to behave in this world, a message very different from what they had heard just a few years before in slavery.

A key element of African American sermons is their identification with the story and struggle in the biblical texts. To be able to make parallels between the enslavement of the Israelites in Egypt and blacks in America, to be able to compare the liberation of the Israelites with the emancipation of the slaves gives meaning and substance to the African American sermon.

> Exposed in depth to the Old Testament, the slaves found it amazingly similar to their traditional faith. There were many parallels, such as the Tower of Babel, a female source of evil, and a deception story quite similar to Jacob's story. The word *tribe* in the Old Testament means extended family society, just as it does in West Africa. They knew God to be just, provident, omnipotent, omniscient. Their praise names for God consisted of these very theological adjectives.[18]

What is important in African American preaching is convincing the listener that God is not only concerned about you in the "sweet by and by," but also concerned about you and involved in your affairs right now. This element is critical for preaching on social issues because it announces

God's action and demonstrates God's involvement in the world.

The African American sermon is a model for preaching on social issues first, because it is deeply biblical preaching. In spite of the fact that the Bible was initially used against them, to keep them in slavery and second-class citizenship, African Americans are people of the book.

> Any understanding of Black preaching must include a sensitivity to the multifaceted Black-culture approach to the Bible, because Black preaching has been centered in the Bible throughout its history. Black congregations do not ask what is a preacher's personal opinion. They want to know what God has said through the preacher's encounter with the Word.[19]

The sermons that have the greatest and most lasting impact are biblical because of the personal experiences and associations of the community of faith with the causes and issues that affect their lives. The preacher who would preach on social issues in the African American context has a listening audience that knows firsthand about oppression and racism, drugs and violence, crime and shrinking social services. This is not to say that other races and ethnic groups have not and do not have these experiences, but that African Americans know what it is like to deal with these issues while still clinging tenaciously to the faith. Preachers who know from experience what it is like to be disenfranchised, decentered, and cut off from the mainstream of life are able to speak on social issues with passion and conviction.

Certainly every preacher will be called upon to engage in some form of social evangelism at one time or another— What an empty and unrewarding ministry any preacher will have if he or she does not dare to tackle these tough issues confronting the contemporary community of faith. But what any other preacher can do by choice, the African American preacher *must* do. Those who make their way to the Black Church gather for retreat and solace; retreat from the harsh realities of being black in America and solace that at some point, something will be said that will get them through the week on their jobs, in the classroom, and at home. Sermons preached in the African American Church must make sense not only for life in the next world but for life in this world.

To make sense of this world calls for a constructive engagement of the realities of this life. In this regard, the African American preacher must be willing to move beyond the "three points and a poem, the hoop and the holler" methodologies. What is needed, indeed, what is required, is thorough exegesis, research, and delivery to communicate God's involvement in this world. Once there is true change in their circumstances and in the world, there will be plenty to celebrate.

WHAT CAN WE SAY TO THESE THINGS?

The Sermon as a Moment of Spiritual Combat in the African American Church Tradition

Mark V. C. Taylor

THE thoughtful observer of the last thirty-five years of American urban reality might well ask the question, "How is it that problems in African American urban communities seem to have worsened since the 1950's and 1960's?" I would answer that question with a question, "Whatever happened to the notion of love in American public discourse?" The notion of love was a major part of the social discourse of the Civil Rights and Black Power movements. The Civil Rights Movement might be considered the first stage of this discourse of "love," while the Black Power Movement's usage of the same concept might be considered its second stage. One answer to this question of "what happened" is that the repression of Black nationalists like the Black Panther Party, and the death of Black nationalists like Malcolm X, meant the social decline of the black nationalist notion of black people loving themselves. The linkage of Martin Luther King's civil rights efforts with antiwar protests, as well as the movement's failure to seriously impact the social and political realities of the urban North, subsumed King's later realization that Negro self-love had to receive greater emphasis in his campaigns.

Post-movement efforts like Jesse Jackson's "I Am Some-body" campaign of Operation Breadbasket and Operation Push, and James Cone's Black Theology were either local-ized in major cites (Jackson's in Chicago) or major institu-tions (Cone's at Union Theological Seminary in New York). The "love discourse" found on the two-way street of African American progressive Christianity was lost on the lonely highway of the systemic counteroffensive's repres-sion and subjugation. Love's decline from visibility in pub-lic discourse did not mean its total demise, however. My major concern in this essay is with those forms of Christian collective love which focused on the African American community loving itself. After all, it was an African Ameri-can evangelical form of communal self-love which birthed the notion of love for enemies and for others found in the Civil Rights Movement.

African American Christian churches had long become the bedrock for the communal profession and practice of love. Historically, they had carried on the discourse of love in four important ways. First they utilized their evangelical teaching and preaching to shape a practice in which a tran-scendent God called forth a community of those despised and rejected in order to create a community where no one would be despised and rejected. This meant that African American churches struggled hard to unite their members across the dividing lines of socioeconomic class. Second, they promoted collective redistribution of wealth through benevolent offerings, tithing, fund-raising, and in-kind giving. Third, they created systems of education and care to facilitate the progress of their members in a hostile world. Fourth, they combined for collective action in the interests of social justice.

When I came to the Church of the Open Door in 1990, I found a congregation that continued this fourfold praxis of love. I found this church to be very committed to the surrounding public housing development, defining the development's welfare as part of its mission. Many of the problems that are associated with urban areas were present in our community: joblessness, drug trafficking and abuse, crime, violence, and disease. Against these, my predecessor and the church had struggled valiantly, but the flood of trouble seemed to be unstoppable.

Besides these problems, four other problems loomed large. First among these were the results of the misguided policies of the federal government, which prevented public housing from reaching its full potential and which inhibited the growth and progress of the existent public housing developments. The history of public housing in America abounds with examples of such policies, from the decision to place housing units in disproportionate concentration in neighborhoods which were already poor, to the deliberate decision to construct public housing units in ways inferior to private rental units as a concession to the urging of lobbies like the National Association of Real Estate Boards (NAREB), to the wage ceilings of the 1949 Housing Act, which called for the forced ejection of the strongest and most stable residents, whose incomes had risen.

The second problem, which very quickly manifested itself in my pastorate, was the social stigma that was, and is, attached to public housing. Once public housing units became mostly African American and Hispanic, and working class and poor (due to the government-sponsored flight of whites to the suburbs), they began to be depicted as the worst places in the city, full of gangs, drugs, and crime.

The myth of the "bad" and "evil" "projects," obscured the social, economic, and political historical forces that shaped public housing's reality. Also obscured was the extent to which public housing developments are *neighborhoods in contention*, that is, neighborhoods characterized by the hotly contested struggle of positive versus negative forces. To eliminate or omit the existence of the positive forces is to omit and eliminate the existence of the majority of people in most public housing developments, who are fine, decent people struggling to create the best possible lives for themselves and their children. To demonize their housing space as the myth of public housing does is to demonize these people. This is precisely what the stigma of public housing does. It is but another version of the argument that any collective of African Americans is inherently pathological. If this is true, the only viable choices open to residents are desperate escape or intoxicating humor, both of which are constantly suggested by print and screen media.

A third enemy encountered in my pastorate was collective depression. This is caused by rampant joblessness and the unrelenting attack against African Americans in all spheres of American life. The systematic assaults on their bodies, the theft of their properties, the educational, journalistic, religious, and legal assaults on their intelligence, humanity and citizenship, have thrown some segments of the African American community into a collective depression.

Homeless persons readily come to mind as examples. But every homeless woman carrying her belongings in a bag and every homeless man carrying his in a shopping cart are the results of a long set of social processes and mental disorders that have encouraged flight from a society that has crushed them again and again and again. Collective depression is the product of social processes that include falsified elections, gerrymandering, redlining, restrictive covenants, and physical assassination. In public housing developments collective depression manifests itself in civic neglect and political apathy, as well as drug addiction and violence.

A final enemy encountered in my pastorate was the challenge of community organizing. Most young adults were, and are, trying to find a career niche or simply land a job. Many youth were, and are, swept up in what Cornel West calls "market culture." This meant that many community struggles were most often led by the senior women of the community. They produced heroic efforts, but against the backdrop of the multitude of social forces arrayed against them, they needed help from other segments of the community. While structural changes in the economy have hurt public housing neighborhoods by moving manufacturing jobs from the community, the manufacturing of chaos through forces like the drug trade, a biased legal system, and an insensitive educational system, damages community cohesion. What can a preacher do against such foes? What can we say to these things? Enter James Melvin Washington.

One of Washington's major concerns was the idea of the acquisition of different modes of spiritual power and their social uses. His written texts analyze the National Baptist Convention movement, the Civil Rights Movement, and prayer as modes of spiritual power that had social uses. He also understood the sermon as a moment of spiritual combat. I remember a conversation we had in 1982 at Union

Theological Seminary. Washington said: "Preaching is like combat. It's like war. The preacher stands on the battlefield and struggles with the enemies of his day, be they sin, evil, meaninglessness, pettiness, or unbelief. The congregation aids the preacher in the struggle by saying, 'amen'; 'un-huh'; 'yes Lord'; 'make it plain'; 'go ahead'; 'say it.' But the main thing for the preacher is to wait on the Lord."

In this understanding, Scripture and preaching were powerful spiritual weapons acquired for the purposes of fighting the good fight of faith. They were good enough for our foreparents and consequently good enough for contemporary believers. This was no new understanding of the preaching task. Indeed, it was old as the biblical account of creation, where God's creative discourses and conversations establish God as the first preacher and preaching, then, as something that comes from God. I think that Washington would argue however, that the best contemporary preaching is forged in the furnace of the intellectually broadest and spiritually deepest investigation possible.

So, the preacher faces the external enemies of government neglect, political indifference, corporate opposition, and social stigmatization. The preacher faces the internal enemies of collective depression and organizing inadequacies. What can she or he say to these things? The preacher has the Word and the preacher can preach the Word. My chief weapon against the obstacles mentioned here was, and is, the pulpit. Luther's notion that preaching is an event in which the Risen Christ is present was helpful to me, because it meant that the Risen Christ was present in the midst of theses difficulties.

The enemies I mentioned have not been vanquished.

They have been defeated momentarily but come roaring back. Our struggles are by no means over. But if one uses the hermeneutical freedom available in most American churches and seeks that intellectually broad and spiritually deep pragmatic response to the problems of our day, a mighty step forward can be made.

My ministry as a preacher in the context described above has prompted the question about "love" in American social discourse, which opens this writing. I think that in our postmodern, pluralistic context, "love" must be resurrected as a central item in the public discourse of African Americans, if no one else. Particularly necessary are progressive Christian formulations of such "love." Progressive evangelical notions of African American communal self-love do not end in ethnocentrism or xenophobia. They must however begin with the depth of the problems created by the overwhelming hatred and scorn poured on African Americans (and all Africans) in the Western world.

Such formulations must be grounded in the hermeneutics of contemporary African American evangelicalism. As long as African American evangelicalism maintains its current silence and timidity on this issue, it will not be able to effectively minister to the unchurched or nonbelievers in the communities surrounding its churches. A progressive evangelical notion of love, complex and mature, extends to the neighbor and the enemy. Too often in African American history the love of neighborhood and enemy has obscured, if not eliminated, the love for the communal self. The first test of such a reformulation of "love" is its ability to address the multitude of problems facing the average African American congregant.

Instead of trying to address this multitude, I want to choose one reoccurring problem which I see in my own work as pastor of a church in a large, urban public housing project. This one problem generates, undergirds, and complicates other problems. It is somewhat difficult to define and discuss. Let us call it the Unholy Spiritual Triumvirate of White Supremacy as manifested in self-destructiveness, self-hatred, and self-doubt.

In regard to this Triumvirate, African American preachers, even in this postmodern era of "multiethnicism" and "diversity," can go back and grasp the tradition of the combative sermon, which emphasized racial advancement. Preachers today find that the words of the great Baptist leader of the 1880s, Rev. C. T. Walker, still ring true:

> The pulpit, fireside and school room are the levers that must lift up our downtrodden race and produce God's glory over creation. . . . The pulpit brings heaven down to earth . . . the Negro must shape his own destiny, solve his own problem, make his own history.[1]

I share the view of those who argue that the practitioners of white supremacy responded vigorously to the challenges of the Civil Rights and Black Power movements. This response both intensified the power of white supremacy and made its existence more difficult to identify and attack. The mutated forms of white supremacy that constituted this response have produced economic relationships, political practices, and social interactions, which in turn produce, especially in working-class and poor black communities, what James Washington called in one of our conversations, a "suicidal impulse motivated by a genocidal thrust."

A serious study of the crime statistics, health reports, prison records, and indigenous media of the populations of these communities reveals self destructiveness, that is, destructive acts by members of the black community, against that community or its members, to be a pressing problem. White supremacy is still a major form of sin and evil in American society, which steals, kills, and destroys. It still ought to be attacked.[2]

Analysis of the minds and the mindset of all Americans have documented the ways in which the negative and positive social meanings attached to the colors black and white, and their symbolic uses and associations in Western society, have justified and fueled the hatred of blacks by whites and the self-hatred of blacks.[3] Continued assaults upon African American intelligence, African American responsibility, and African American beauty occur in academic texts and popular media.[4] When these attacks are linked to the deathly play of other economic, political, and cultural forces operating both consciously and unconsciously under the dictates of white supremacy, radical self-doubt becomes a feature of life in the African American community. We doubt if we are at home in this country. We doubt who and what we are, and what we can be.

What can the preacher say to these things? In order to combat each item in the Unholy Spiritual Triumvirate of White Supremacy (self-doubt, self-hatred, self-destructiveness), the preacher can find in the Scriptures, an underutilized text, a controversial "sermonic idea" and a pragmatic goal.[5] To combat one element of this Triumvirate is to combat them all. Let us examine a sermonic counterattack against the self-doubt socially induced by white supremacy.

Jeremiah 29:11–14
For I know the plans I have for you, says the Lord, plans for welfare and not for evil, to give you a future and a hope. [12] Then you will call upon me and come

and pray to me, and I will hear you. [13] You will seek
me and find me when you seek me with all your heart.
[14] I will be found by you, says the Lord, and I will re-
store your fortunes and gather you from all the nations
where I have driven you, says the Lord, and I will bring
you back to the place from which I sent you into exile.
(Revised Standard Version)[6]

Preaching against self-doubt, the preacher can turn to
Jeremiah 29:11–14, and preach "God's Plan for 'I' and
'We.'" The sermonic or central idea of this sermon is that
in spite of the ravages of sin and evil in human life, each of
us had a Divine destiny in the mind of God before the
world began. If we rely on the future that just naturally
comes to us or that others or we make ourselves, then we
will wind up in despair. The texts tell us that God gives the
faithful their future. It is that God-given future that produces hope. Such a future is grounded in the spiritual
praxis of seeking God with every aspect of one's being.
When an individual or group seeks God's plan, God's future, and God, God's self, then health and blessings are restored to it. The pragmatic goal of this sermon is to help
individuals and groups see themselves as special recipients
of Divine love and attention because God had, and has, a
plan for them. Part of this goal is to implant a new sense of
self-esteem that produces individual stability and group
unity.

Now let us examine a sermonic counterattack against
the self-hatred socially induced by white supremacy.

Romans 9:1–3
I am speaking the truth in Christ, I am not lying; my con-
science bearing me witness in the Holy Spirit, [2] that
I have great sorrow and unceasing anguish in my heart.

[3] For I could wish that I myself were accursed and cut
off from Christ for the sake of my brethren, my kinsmen
by race.

Romans 10:1
Brethren, my heart's desire and prayer to God for them is
that they may be saved.

Preaching against self-hatred, the preacher can turn to
Romans 9:1–3, and Romans 10:1 and preach "Do You Love
Your People?" The sermonic idea of this sermon is that the
encounter with Christ prompts and propels believers into
a witness that helps them to see their own people with new
insight and new compassion. It compels believers to wrestle with the special forms of sin and evil that plague the inner and outer spaces occupied by their race, and to search
for the specific forms of ministry called for in the salvation
of Jesus Christ for their deliverance.

The pragmatic goal of this sermon is to help hearers to
see through the lens of communion with Christ, the beauty
and blessedness of each of the "families of the earth," especially their own "family," which has been symbolically and
culturally degraded by the doctrines of white supremacy.
Another part of this goal is for such love to motivate the defining of African American interests and the ability to *more*
successfully negotiate the pursuit of those interests in the
major systems of American society, for example, the fi-
nancial system, the educational system, the criminal justice
system, the political system, and the real estate system. Finally, let us turn our attention to a sermonic counterattack
against the self-destructiveness socially induced as part of
the Unholy Spiritual Triumvirate of White Supremacy.

I Corinthians 16:9
. . . for a wide door for effective work has opened to me,
and there are many adversaries.

Preaching against self-destruction, the preacher can turn to I Corinthians 16:9 and preach, "Social Crisis is Spiritual Opportunity." The sermonic idea here is that the economic, political, and social structures arrayed against the African American community are great but the resources of spiritual power available to the faithful are greater. These resources include the Word of God, the Spirit of God, the Church of God, the Power of God, and the spiritual legacy of our parents and elders. The path of spiritual accomplishment and achievement, however, is filled with adversaries. But there is no salvation, no healing, no deliverance, no blessing, no restoration, no progress without a sacrificial struggle.

The pragmatic goal of this sermon is to develop within the faithful an unshakable conviction that the plethora of present problems cannot negate the opportunity God gives to act and thereby shape reality, to act and thereby create truth, to act and thereby become a vessel of the Divine will. Alongside this conviction, another goal is the acceptance of the belief that effective Christian witness means being able and willing to put oneself on the line (i.e., at risk) in the struggle for social transformation.

These examples of underutilized texts, controversial sermonic ideas, and pragmatic goals are meant to be suggestive rather than exhaustive. Many other texts and strongholds of human oppression could have been mentioned as examples here. I have purposely omitted many questions of exegesis, hermeneutics, and traditional homiletics. The point of these omissions was to highlight the understanding of the sermon as a form of spiritual combat. This is just one illustration of the path that a contemporary combative homiletics concerned with human emancipation might take.

Such sermons are not substitutes for action against the structures of oppression, however. No text, no sermon, no artistic production or rendition can substitute for the moment of direct action against the structures that oppress and destroy. However, sermons like those suggested above can help people experience that Ultimate Reality we confess as Jesus Christ and thereby receive power to challenge these sinful and evil realities on the face of the earth.

Preaching by Punctuation

Moving from Texts and Ideas to Sermons
That Live with Passion

Gary V. Simpson

I BEGIN with a confession. I have considered writing about preaching for some time now, but I have been very leery of doing so. I have not yet crystallized my own ideas. It will, perhaps, take a lifetime to do that. In addition, there is an abundance of books on the subject. "How to . . . , "How do *you* . . . , anthologies, collections and series. In addition, ours is the age of larger-than-life images transported to us by radio and television stations across the world. Our image of "good preaching" is shifting dramatically. The determination of what a good preacher sounds like has more to do with how many stations cover one's worship service. I fear that what I have to say on this subject might be judged in that context by those realities.

We live in a visually based culture that the French philosopher Jacques Ellul has aptly described as an age of "the humiliation of the word."[1] The air is filled with pop culture's exaggerated caricature of the preacher, preaching, and African American religious life in general. The pop diva Madonna begs her father, "Poppa Don't Preach," while the raspy timbre and rhythm of the black preacher's voice is more often used by hip-hoppers and would-be love balladeers only to seduce their listeners into temporarily satisfied moments of fleeting pleasures. A recently aired made-for-television movie was marketed as "the untold story" of the Buffalo Soldiers, black cavalry soldiers who played a significant part in the westward expansion of the United States after the Civil War. There was a funeral scene in which the black soldiers gathered around the grave of a fallen comrade. The movie has these nineteenth-century Buffalo Soldiers singing "Precious Lord," even though the prolific African American composer Thomas Dorsey did not write the song until 1938! This cultural backdrop calls for us to hear anew the challenge issued by the Apostle Paul to his young protégé, Timothy: "Preach the word in season and out of season," for one would believe that preachers, as critical interpreters of the Word of God, appear to be out of season.

I am intentionally an expository preacher. I understand that the implication of such a moniker carries with it much baggage. Expository preaching is more than the caricature of holding the Bible in one hand and pointing a finger at sinners with the other. I do assert that there is no preaching that does not begin with, and rise up out of, contact and intersection with the biblical witness. One cannot assume that either the preacher or the congregation is fluent in biblical languages and nuance. The simple task of the sermon is to proclaim truth about Christ. The best working definition of black preaching I have found is in Frank Thomas's *They Like to Never Quit Praisin' God*. Thomas contends that "the nature and purpose of black preaching is to get the listener to encounter grace. That is the gospel of Jesus Christ."[2]

This definition suffices to establish the core of our work. Nonetheless, there is so much teaching about the biblical witness that needs to be done. An important task for the contemporary preacher is to have his or her listeners discover the meaning of timeless biblical truths and confessions about Jesus Christ.

In *The Teaching Minister*, Clark Williams and Ronald Allen assert that "everything teaches in the ministry and in the church." In reality, the church community and culture are one of didactic relationships and symbols. As this is the case, "the central work of the minister is to be a theologian who reflects critically on the appropriateness, intelligibility and the morality of the Christian witness even while making that witness."[3]

In this essay, I propose a way of looking at sermon development as intricately tied to "creative process." Then I will suggest a structure of organization for this creativity by using the marks of punctuation (periods, question marks, and exclamation points, specifically) as a means of developing a sense of sermon movement.

Preparing the Sermon: Creative Moments and Movements

When I describe the preaching craft, I make the grand (and I hope not careless) presupposition that preaching is both textual and contextual. To fail to present both in a sermon is mere façade or sleight of hand. A distinction should be drawn between reckless, careless work and innovative, creative preaching. Creativity connotes a thorough understanding of the craft. All the great innovators in the arts are first students of their historic predecessors. Truly creative spirits are not self-defined as the antithesis or supersession of that which came before. A good practitioner in any discipline is first and foremost a student of the discipline.

Take, for example, jazz as innovative practice. As a genre of musical expression, jazz is perhaps best known for its use of improvisation. Improvisation, however, is not without nod to form. In fact, how does one understand the term "improvisation" without first understanding the structure, form, space, and timing of a performance? The great jazz innovators of our era—John Coltrane, Duke Ellington, and Winton Marsalis, to name a few—all possessed a great understanding of the rules, forms, and movements within their musical discipline; then as innovators they pressed the boundaries.

It is unfortunate that much of contemporary preaching is anachronistic. Ask a preacher who her or his heroes of the discipline are and perhaps one may mention one or two living people, and likely with an accompanying television broadcast. We are not aware of the giants of the craft, like John Jasper, Jarena Lee, Washington Taylor, Julia Foote, Florence Spearing Randolph, L. K. Williams, J. C. Austin, Sandy Ray, Sam Proctor, and Gardner Taylor. Beyond this specific inheritance, we are also heirs to a global tradition of Wesley, Chrysostom, McClaren, Spurgeon, Bernard of Clairvaux, and many others. It is not enough to abscond with their messages and mimic their mannerisms. We are called to immerse our whole being into this life-giving artistry. A good preacher must know the craft.

Quite frankly, it is nearly impossible to pin down the task of preaching to a science or system. It is at once artistic creation and definable method. Preaching is the manifestation of interdisciplinary thinking. According to the late Samuel DeWitt Proctor, our task is "to track out (down) a sermon as does a hunting dog." Ideas flood the preacher's conscious from everywhere—life experience, current readings, social pathos, scriptural discoveries, devotional reflections, and personal memories. How does the preacher process these ideas and shape them into a form that gives life? There are a plethora of resources available beyond the discipline of homiletics. In his book, *Creativity*, the psychologist Mihaly Csikszentmihalyi argues that the creative process has five critical movements. These ideas can be transposed onto the sermon movement.

The first movement is *preparation*. Csikszentmihalyi describes this step as the process of "becoming immersed consciously in a set of problematic issues that are interesting and arouse curiosity."[4] In the preparation of sermons, this is the deliberate tracking of possible ideas and themes in scripture and in life experience. True preparation begins in the devotional life of the preacher and in one's ability to listen to and translate mundane human experiences and events into eternally meaningful insights. In biblical language, what feeds the shepherd who feeds the sheep? James A. Forbes told our introductory Homiletics course at Union Seminary of New York, "Don't spend Saturday night lusting after texts to preach on Sunday." In other words, the preacher must be committed to a life that provides the appropriate setting and climate for receiving and pondering ideas. This cannot happen if the only contact with the life and faith of the church is spent developing something to say before a congregation. To this end, every preacher should keep a file of notes and ideas.

The second movement is *incubation*. "As ideas churn around the threshold of consciousness, unusual connections and associations are made. These ideas call back and forth to each other."[5] Some ideas are not immediately ready for preaching. Contexts and text arise to court one another before they are wed. The preacher is to ponder the world of the biblical witness and happenings in the current world. For example, one of my favorite stories is that of Luke 15, the parable of the Prodigal Son. Let us ponder that text in the late twentieth-century context of single parents, preoccupation with maleness (sexism), and issues of the viable economic future of families. What are the possible intersections between these two worlds? Pondering subtle nuances releases a world of homiletic possibility.

A certain man had two sons . . .

A certain man had two sons . . .
    Is Mr. Certain a single parent?

A *certain* man had two sons . . .
    Does this story lose its emphasis in our traditional
    reading of the text? Is this story about the child or
    the parent?

A certain *man* had two sons . . .
    Where is Mrs. Certain? And what would happen to
    the family's divided wealth if we changed "man" to
    "woman," given what we know about single-female-
    headed households?

A certain man *had* two sons . . .
    What is the responsibility of parenting? Is it enough
    to "possess" children? What about the possibility of
    prodigal parents?

A certain man had *two sons* . . .
    Have we again only assigned worth to the male chil-
    dren? What would happen if the gender of these boys
    was changed? Would the outcome be the same?

A certain man had two sons . . .
    Is there good news waiting at this juncture of the
    text? Can we prevent this sermon from making its
    usual preoccupation with the prodigal son's "worldli-
    ness" and offer hope to the parent (children) of prodi-
    gals today?

The third movement is *insight*. What are some particular and specific insights or experiences that help inform and shape a sermon? As the sermon is at once a word of testimony to the truth of the past (particularly the biblical witness), it is also a word of revelation, of keenly relevant insight into the present situation before God and with each other in community. What does God have at stake or invested in this word today?

This leads to the fourth movement, which is *evaluation*. Is this idea worth pursuing? Is it valuable? Not enough of the preacher's time is spent asking this kind of question. The basis of evaluating a sermon in the making is the preacher's use of heart, mind, soul, and spirit. Restated, what is this sermon's passion *index*? By this phrase, I mean to ask: a) what is the preacher's investment of the core of his/her being in the proclamation of this particular word? Is she/he convinced of the truth of the proposed message? b) Has the preacher made best use of resources and data for information as a scholar/student of the word? c) Does the sermon have any relevant connection to the lives of people? d) Is there present a spiritual integrity connected to the heritage of the faithful?

The final movement is *elaboration*. An idea becomes a sermon at this point. It manifests itself in the writing and thinking through of these conceptual pathways. The preacher must be cautioned not to think that these five movements have a linear relationship. As Csikszentmihalyi aptly assesses, this process is recursive. During this part of the process, some suggested form, style, and even rhythm is probed, always keeping the listeners in mind.

Perhaps the most difficult challenge for the preacher is to shape this creative process into a public presentation that will last a specified amount of time. How does one move from concept to design? From formulations to form?

When describing what form a sermon takes, what it looks like, "movement" is more consistent with the process than "points." Points suggest too linear a relationship and too cerebral an exercise. The term "movement" suggests more than logical sequence. It suggests flow, pace, pathos, and rhythm. The remainder of this essay will be devoted to describing the movements of a soundly structured sermon.

Preaching Power for the New Millennium: Implosion or Explosion?

It is a very exciting time to be a preacher. On the edge of a new millennium, we own the privilege of being able to proclaim the last word for Christ in the twentieth century and issuing the first herald of the twenty-first century. We have the awesome task of looking forward to the soul's thirst and search for meaning in the twenty-first century. Regrettably, in this era of gleeful anticipation, much of our preaching is rather unexciting. There is too much "comma preaching." Boring and dysfunctional. We have all heard it going on and continuing like one long sentence: point 1, point 2, point 3 . . .

This reality is connected to our current preoccupation with lists and points. Such preoccupation tends to give us a very quick and shallow assessment of the priorities of our lives. The complexity of the human struggle cannot always be neatly reduced to alliterative descriptions and "top ten" lists. The soul urges, yearns for something that digs deep enough to establish meaning or a *raison d'être*. As Henry Mitchell and Frank Thomas both assert, a sermon must also tap into the emotive consciousness of the listener.

This is not to say that our contemporary preaching is

not "excitable." On the other side of the spectrum, there is preaching that is geared only toward the emotions, that searches for a particular ecstatic response from the hearers. In many places, the standards for listening and assessing a sermon's power today are based on feeling, not passion.

Much of our preaching is more like the intentional demolition of dilapidated buildings done by skilled construction workers, who meticulously and strategically place dynamite throughout an old, unusable and unstable structure at key stress points. If this is done correctly, an implosion causes the old building to fall in on itself with minimal impact to the adjacent structures. This is the danger of purely celebrative intentions. Sermons are prepared, shaped, and structured to cause the church to fall, only collapsing on itself. Just listen to the language we use to describe powerful sermons. "I tore the house up!" "S/he slayed them." "S/he wrecked the building!" Is this the value of a life-giving word? It appears that such language is antithetical to the preaching task. The difference between implosion and explosion is simple: an implosion is a falling inward due to external pressure; an explosion is a falling outward based on internal pressure. The task of preaching is to rouse up, turn up the internal force to cause the church to fall outside itself with unimagined energy and impact.

Periods, Question Marks, and Exclamation Points: The Grammar of Sermon Movement

In order to have this explosion take place, I propose that we capitalize on the simple nuances and lessons of our language. Simply stated, I propose that we allow the grammar lessons of childhood to wake up our preaching. I am often rescued in moments of grammatical uncertainty by the lessons I learned watching a Saturday morning television segment called "Schoolhouse Rock":

> *Interjection!*
> *Shows emotion or excitement*
> *It's generally set apart from a sentence by an*
> *exclamation point*
> *Or by a comma when the feeling's not as strong!*

Here, then, is a suggested process for structuring the sermon:

(.) The Statement. Gardner Taylor was once asked in a homiletics class at Harvard exactly how many points there should be in a sermon. His reply was, "Well, at least one." The sermon idea should be able to be stated in some clear and concise form. Samuel Proctor often asked his students, "What will you have said when you will have said it?" Too much preaching lacks a clearly stated focus and seems to flow from nontributary streams of consciousness. Whereas stream of consciousness is a good method for distilling sermon ideas, it is cumbersome as a method of sermon delivery because the listener cannot follow the preacher's movement. To combat this problem, the preacher must have a statement that summarizes the central topic of the sermon. Although this sentence does not have to be stated at the time of sermon delivery—for example, "Today I am going to talk with you about the unconditional love of God"— such a statement must be clearly in the head of the preacher who plans to use this idea as a guiding theme.

Preaching is, at its root, declaration, proclamation. Without certainty at this place, a sermon is doomed to wander aimlessly. Going back to the Prodigal Son passage from Luke 15; a sermon-defining statement might look like any one of these:

- There is hope for single parents.
- Parents and children must work together for family wholeness.
- Selfishness within families can be conquered by unconditional love.

Establishing this clear sentence now challenges and charges the preacher to return to this central idea throughout the sermon structure. At some level, everything within the sermon must connect back to this central proclamation.

(?) The Tide of Questions. In approaching the text and the idea of a sermon, one must enter into the process of query. No statement ever made at any time is accepted completely by everyone who hears it. The preacher lives and prepares, as best he or she can, in anticipation of the questions asked in the pews. Many of these questions, but certainly not all of them, are in our own minds if we are honest. At best then, any statement we make in preaching is a faith statement. At any given point, the "substance of things hoped for" is challenged, contradicted, and oftentimes seemingly conquered by the "seen" evidence of the present world. On the other hand, this questioning is somewhat akin to Proctor's transferring of Hegelian phenomenology to the methodology of sermon crafting. Whereas Proctor argues that a single relevant question is the query on which the sermon hinges, there is a flood of questions raised by the search for truth in knowledge that together shape the sermon as a symphony. Here are a few essential questions:

- Why is this declaration important at this particular time?
- In making this statement, what am I saying about
  my beliefs about the God and the divine encounter with the world?
- What are my own theological stakes in this text
  and this word?
- What are the living contradictions in the life of
  the congregation and community that keep this
  from being the word of life for this moment?
- What have others said about this text or idea?
- How does this sermon connect to the life of the
  hearer?

Here are a few biblical questions to be asked to the text
for preaching:

- What is the form and structure of the text?
- In what "biblical neighborhood" does the text
  live?
- Do I agree with the faith claims presented here?
- What is my gut reaction to the text?
- What voice or approach does this text speak to me
  in?
- What is the location of the "good news" in this
  particular passage?

(!) *The Point of Emphasis*. If the sermon survives our own
questioning, we are then again moved to restate the statement more emphatically. What began as a simple statement
and survives a battery of questions and challenges emerges
as a point of passion at the sermon's conclusion.

Here I take a sharp turn from Henry Mitchell's notion
of the climactic moment of black preaching as a place of

celebration.[6] Although I think Mitchell's analysis is much deeper than mere jubilation, celebration remains a very dangerous idea in the contemporary church. Celebration refers to the climactic euphoria at the end of the sermon. Certainly, proclamation must take place, but it is not always an act of celebration. Within the Psalms, the Hebrew praise book, there is the proclamation of pain and suffering, as well as joy and adoration. A continuous focus on praise and worship alone does not convey the panoramic view of the divine encounter we know as Scripture. When the eccentric evangelist John the Baptist proclaimed in the wilderness, "Repent, for the kingdom of God is at hand!," that was not a moment for celebration and dance. A more appropriate response would be to fall on one's knees in woe and to rise in the rite of forgiveness called baptism.

Of course the task of preaching is not to provide the answers but to proclaim Christ. As a child, I was an avid reader of *MAD* magazine. Al Jaffe had a recurring contribution entitled "Snappy Answers to Stupid Questions." Sometimes a preacher must conclude with a passionate "I do not know!" There is also the possibility that a sermon could end with a passionate question. Irrespective of the actual punctuation of a final point or movement in a sermon, it must be given in the passionate spirit. There are appropriate corresponding ideas of impassioned silence. A sermon does not have to end loudly (referring to the decibels of the voice). There are moments when a preacher must lead the congregation to those places of a deafening silence for their own passionate introspection. Sometimes the "noise" of a loud voice in the pulpit is a distraction from the shouts of the inner voice. What is the driving point of the text and one's wrestling with it? Here the preacher has the opportunity to rehearse, recount, retell, and reaffirm the deeper, lasting truths of God. In any passage, however, there are many competing words that could be preached. The where and how are shaped by the . , ? and ! of the preacher.

One of my lasting memories is a bus trip sponsored by the Twin Five Circle in the church of my youth. Every year, they would take the eleven-hour bus ride to Bloomington, Illinois, to see the American Passion Play. It appeared that the entire town got involved in some aspect of the production and people from hundreds of miles in every direction would come to see the masterful performance. Scenes like the Sermon on the Mount and Jesus walking on water came alive before the very eyes of an impressionable fourteen-year-old.

To preserve the sacred nature of the performance, the audience was asked to refrain from flash pictures, audio-visual recording, and excessive talking during the production. The play ascended to the powerful resurrection scene, in which an angel swooped down and rolled the massive stone from the mouth of the sepulchre. Absolutely breath-taking! Suddenly, two rows in front of our section, an older African American woman instinctively shouted, "He's out! He's out!" She broke all manner and semblance of decorum without restraint. "He's out! He's out!" The usher hurried over and whispered to her, I am sure reminding her of the theater's policy about talking during the performance. To this the woman replied, "I know! But He's out! He's out!"

Wow! What a sermon she preached that day! This is the essence of preaching.

It is the unrestrainable passion to tell the good news of Christ. It is when a *statement*

Jesus rose. (Preparation, Incubation, Insight, Evaluation, Elaboration)

becomes a *query,*

Jesus rose? (Preparation, Incubation, Insight, Evaluation, Elaboration)

becomes a *passion,*

Jesus rose!!!

becomes a sermon worth hearing.

HAVE YOU NOT READ WHAT
DAVID DID?

A Sermon for Jim Washington

Richard Newman

I MET James Melvin Washington over twenty years ago at the Northeast Seminar on Black Religion, a small but faithful group founded by Preston Williams with a core membership that included Randall Burkett, Al Raboteau, Ed Redkey, David Wills, and Jim. We met four times a year, usually in Cambridge, New Haven, New York, and Princeton, to hear a paper, engage in good conversation, catch up on the news, and eat lunch together. For people often working in isolation on African American religion, the Seminar was a providential place to talk and listen, learn and discuss, and, most important, have one's own work-in-progress both understood and taken seriously.

Over the years, Jim and I shared other interests: the tangled internal politics of Union Seminary; rare books; our loving regard for Union's extraordinary chaplain, Lee Hancock; the neglect of black Baptist history; obscure bibliographic sources and references; and the fact that Patricia Sullivan's book *Days of Hope: Race and Democracy in the New Deal Era* (1996) includes a photograph of a political rally for Progressive Party presidential candidate Henry Wallace at Jim's beloved home church, Mt. Olive Baptist in Knoxville, a photograph taken the year Jim was born and in which I am visible in a corner of the sanctuary.

162

We also shared, often with an eye toward publication, an interest in collecting and compiling. I had a contract with Macmillan for a book of Martin Luther King, Jr.'s sermons and articles, but Mrs. King, who held the rights, finally refused permission. She did grant permission to Jim (through, he said, "the Baptist connection"), and I happily turned over my files. The result was his wonderful book *A Testament of Hope: The Essential Writings of Martin Luther King, Jr.* (1986), now not only the standard source for Dr. King's essays, but a far better and more important book than anyone else could have done.

I did not know, until it was mentioned at Jim's funeral, that he was a night-time walker through the deserted halls of Union as well as a nocturnal, if technically unauthorized, user of Burke Library. I did know that he once considered compiling a collection of sermons, as he actually did of prayers. In some obscure archive he found the text of an even more obscure sermon I had preached forty years ago. He sent me a copy with a "Look what I found!" note and a generous comment. In rereading it, I see how it reflects its time: the sexist language, the critique of the conformity of the 1950s, the oblique reference to abortion, the Barthian influence, the emphasis on morality over law, obviously effected by Martin Luther King. Despite its youthful limitations, I have decided to include it in this volume as a loving tribute to Jim Washington for several reasons, not least of which is that he chose it himself.

Have You Not Read What David Did?

At that time Jesus went through the grainfields on the sabbath; his disciples were hungry, and they began to pluck ears of grain and to eat. But when the Pharisees saw it, they said to him, "Look, your disciples are doing

what is not lawful to do on the sabbath." He said to
them, "Have you not read what David did, when he was
hungry, and those who were with him: how he entered
the house of God and ate the bread of the Presence
which it was not lawful for him to eat nor for those who
were with him, but only for the priests? Or have you not
read in the law how on the sabbath the priests in the temple profane the sabbath and are guiltless? I tell you something greater than the temple is here. And if you had
known what this means, 'I desire mercy, and not sacrifice,' you would not have condemned the guiltless. For
the Son of man is lord of the sabbath."   Matthew 12: 1–8

This New Testament story is a curious one. Curious,
because we expect Jesus to personify obedience and faithfulness and religiosity; we expect him to be law-abiding,
particularly in terms of the divine commandments. But our
expectations are brought up short, for what confronts us in
this story is a Jesus who defies the religious law and sets
himself over against religious people and religious institutions which uphold that law. And not only does Jesus violate the law, but he dares to use for justification one who occupied for his hearers something of the same status and
authority Jesus occupies for us, another whose righteousness is presupposed: David the king.

The sabbath laws are not merely some human invention. It is God himself who rests on the sabbath and who
sets aside the sabbath in holiness in so that his children can
rest from their work. "It is not Israel which has kept the
sabbath," Abraham Heschel tells us, "but the sabbath
which has kept Israel." So it is no casual thing to defy this
law. Certainly there is no great burden here from which
men cry out to be liberated, for it is a joyful thing to be able
to observe the commandments of God. And Jesus' defense
is as shocking as his irreligious act—"Have you not read

what David did?"—using against the Pharisees the authority of one of whom God said, "I will make him the first-
born."

We cannot question the authority of Jesus for us any
more easily than the Pharisees could question the authority of David for them. So we must be as puzzled as the
Pharisees when we hear the One whom we understand as
a special bearer of revelation saying that the laws of God
are not absolute or binding. This is a strange and unlikely
position for the One whom we would assume to be the
most rigorously, the most totally, the most literally faithful
in their observance. Yet David and Jesus, the great central
figures of Jewish and Christian history, the prototypes of
God's involvement with men, are here both revealed as vio-
lators of the law! What can this mean?

There is a necessarily conservative nature built into all
the institutions which interweave to form a society. Human
society is built upon stability and continuity and predictability. Religious institutions are probably the most conservative of all, since it is these institutions which carry the
very basic beliefs and values upon which the whole society
is constructed. If these beliefs or ways of doing things were
to be altered lightly, then the foundation of the society itself
would be weakened and human self-understanding and
self-confidence would be threatened.

Sociologically, then, one can maintain that a society
cannot survive unless its members share a common culture, and politically one can argue that if every man has a
veto power over the law on the basis of conscience or anything else, then there is no law and men live not in society
but in chaotic anarchy. Obviously, the Bible is not a book
of sociology or government or of religion, for the Word of

God which speaks through it is a living reality which places itself over against every institutionalized cultural form: "Have you not read what David did?"

God speaks a living Word and our human nature forces us to seize that moment of revelation and write it down, institutionalize it, formalize it, structure it, construct a fence around it, build a monument on top of it. And we proudly and triumphantly say, "Here is this Word and we have captured it, and it now belongs to us, and we venerate it." But at just that point it is no longer alive! By trying to possess a living reality we destroy it. Instead of building a church we have built a museum. Instead of hearing a disturbing Word we imprison God's voice in the most respectable of books. Instead of following the Christ we put him under glass and tiptoe up to the showcase to worship, hoping, if we have heard anything at all, that he does not escape.

Gabriel Vahanian has said that "faith necessarily produces religion; religion necessarily destroys faith." It is so. If faith is our response to God's encounter, then our temptation is to try to perpetuate that meeting. So we organize a committee and write a constitution and formulate a ritual and build a building—but that is no longer faith; it is now religion. That which is alive has been snuffed out; that which is vital and vibrant has been crushed under the weight of institutions and formality and tradition. Do we think God's Word is perpetuated by these forms of ours? Do we not know that he does his own speaking? Do we not comprehend that we force him to break through the very structures we have built if his voice is to be heard rather than our voices? "Have we not read what David did?"

H. Richard Niebuhr writes that "institutions can never conserve without betraying the movement from which they proceed." The Word of God, spoken in a creative moment of juncture between the human and the divine, is institutionalized and thus deadened and destroyed. It becomes built into the religious and cultural apparatus, and its radical nature is prostituted into serving the most conservative impulses of human society. The living law of God is absolutized and its animated character is supplanted by an uninspired, dispirited subservience to the letter rather than the spirit, to the law itself rather than the living God who gives the law.

Jesus breaks into this whole institutionalized structure by asking which is more important, the mechanical application of the regulation, or the hunger of David and his men? the technically of the law or the needs of Jesus and his disciples? The answer is clear: the needs of men come before legality and tradition, before theological or ecclesiastical correctness, before the requisites of society and culture. "The sabbath was made for man, not man for the sabbath." Laws are not ends in themselves; they are a means for serving men. It is man as the child of God who is to be served even by God's law, let alone laws and institutions of societal invention.

Laws which fail to serve the needs of men are not only irrelevant to the human situation, then, but they are wrong in the eyes of God, God gives his law for the strengthening of the human community, but when the community perverts that law by making it rigid and inflexible and an end in itself, then God must intervene and speak out for disobedience and violation, that the needs of men might be met and the glory of God truly honored. God will not tolerate the stringent enforcement of laws either sacred or secular which do not aid and assist men.

What is God's response if men are hungry because of laws? If men are without decent places to live because of laws? if there are children who are cold or uneducated or who have no future for development and fulfillment because of laws? if a girl with an unborn and unwanted child must suffer because of laws? if a man who is poor and black must bear indignities and frustration in a society which is white and rich because of laws written or unwritten? What is God's response and what is our response? "Have you not read what David did?" Have you not heard what Jesus did? how he broke the law of God to satisfy, yes, the immediate and physical needs of his disciples? "I am not come to destroy the law but to fulfill."

And Jesus' iconoclasm dares go even beyond this violation. "Something greater than the temple is here." Jesus is saying that it is not only this particular sabbath law he is willing to set aside, but even the temple itself. Even the great structure manifesting the ritual obedience of God's people, where every day the elaborate ceremonies of sacrifice symbolize the devotion of the faithful. Even something greater than that is here in the midst of us—a hungry man! Can it be that God is more interested in the feeding of one hungry man than he is in temples and rituals and ceremonies and legal observances and cultic faithfulness? Is nothing of ours safe from his judgment?

Jesus quotes Hosea: "For I desire steadfast love and not sacrifice, the knowledge of God rather than burnt offerings." Steadfast love is strong, binding, persistent; it connotes mutuality, contract, covenant; it involves response and reciprocity; it goes beyond fidelity and thus finally becomes suffering love. And knowledge is not rational thinking, or correct ideas, or academic speculation, but relationship, intimacy, the involvement of one whole person with another. This is what God wants, not ritual offerings or formalized sacrifices.

Do we naively imagine that Jesus does not speak this Word to us? Do we seriously believe that we are not legalists? that we do not have our own versions, however sophisticated, of the sabbath law? that we do not live on our own little religious requirements and conventions? that we are not entrapped in all the cultural institutionalism of laws and traditions both sacred and secular? that we do not subvert human needs to structures and channels and proper forms? that we do not believe we are obeying God when we are merely products and perpetrators of our religion and society? It is to us that Jesus speaks his Word: "Have you not read what David did?"

Finally, there is at stake in this story not only the divine protest against religion and institutionalism, as well as the fact that human needs come before legal requirements, but the question of true obedience to God. Really, this is a story that provides a clue to the nature of the Messianic age. That is to say, when God's reign begins, then men are able to transcend regulation and convention. Obedience is to God himself rather than to laws, as men live in the radical freedom of the Kingdom. The Kingdom is God's gift, but as it breaks into human history, we catch a glimpse of how life under God is really to be lived.

In another context, Kierkegaard makes this clear in his explanation of Abraham's sacrifice of Isaac. The commandment enjoins men from murder, but Abraham in response to God's direct command takes Isaac his son, the hope of the future, up on the mountain, fully prepared to kill him. Ethics are suspended for the higher end and purpose of true obedience to God's living command. When men live under God's Rule then it is his voice alone which is authoritative. When men live under God's Rule then religion and law are abandoned for a true freedom where men are fully human and a true humanism where men are fully free.

If we would be really faithful then it is to God himself we must respond, not to the laws of either religion or society, not to the institutions of either church or state. God himself is always above these, always beyond, transcendent, other—speaking his clear Word to those who have ears to hear, calling men to be obedient to him rather than all the other voices, good and bad, which tempt us and seduce us and call for our loyalty: "For the Son of man is lord of the sabbath." He calls us to be faithful to him alone, to live in the radical freedom that goes beyond all laws and institutions, all religions and all cultures—the live, vital relationship between God as he is and us as we are.

Through all our pieties and presuppositions, through all the conventions of our life, God's Word comes breaking in: "Have you not read what David did?"

CHURCH &
COMMUNITY

STRANGERS AND THE HOMECOMING

Church and Community in the Grammar of Faith

Dale T. Irvin

A MONG the recurring themes in early Christian literature, one of the more common tropes concerns the status of Christians as strangers in the world. Christians often referred to themselves as *paroikoi*, a word that can be translated as "strangers," "sojourners," or "aliens." It referred to people of a different household (*oikos*), people whose identity was nonresidential.[1] I Peter 2:11 refers to believers as *paroikous kai parepidemous* (strangers and exiles). In the second century, pastoral letters of Clement of Rome and Polycarp of Smyrna were both addressed to the strangers residing at Corinth and Philippi. An anonymous letter from the second or third century, addressed to one named Diognetus, provides us with a fuller grammar for understanding the designation. Offering an explanation of Christian life and practice, the author wrote:

> For the Christians are distinguished from other people neither by land, nor language, nor customs; for they do not inhabit cities of their own, nor use a particular language, nor lead a life that is unusual. . . . But inhabiting Hellenistic as well as barbarian cities, according to each person's lot . . . they display to us their wonderful and admittedly paradoxical (*paradoxon*) way of life. They inhabit their home lands (*patridas*), but as strangers (*paroichoi*). . . . Every foreign land (*xene*) is their home land (*patris*), and every home land a foreign land.[2]

It is a striking trope played out in many different ways in the history of Christian spirituality ever since; followers of Jesus are (or are to be) people who are foreigners, aliens, sojourners in the world. But paradoxically, it is their same "strangerhood" that joins them together in a community.

At times, the literature of this spirituality of "strangerhood" seems intent upon seeking to "unhome" those who are its readers, to make them uneasy with their way of being in the world. Other times it appears that the literature is more reflective of the existential condition of its subjects. In those cases, the narrative of Jesus and his resurrection offers a compelling story of homecoming that can sustain a people through their experience of alienation. Usually it is a mixture of both that the reader encounters, the prescriptive and descriptive dimensions of strangerhood being more or less intermingled in any given time or place. Always the purpose is not to celebrate homelessness but to alert one to the homecoming Christians have before them, as a promise and a memory of the One who went before them.

Few individuals have grappled so intently and intensely with the questions of being at home and being a stranger in the context of modernity as has James Melvin Washington. Throughout his life, throughout his scholarly career, it was his passion to come to grips with the alienations (and they are multiple) of the modern age. Washington often returned to the fundamental problems raised by the "homeless mind" of modernity,[3] doing so from a perspective he called "the sub-modern." Of particular concern for Washington was the collective historical experience of peoples of African descent who through four hundred years of physical oppression, economic exploitation, and psychological degradation suffered the ignominy and the terror of being rendered strangers in what was and was not their own homeland. He grappled with the absurdity and the nihilism that confront one in the modern world, but he did not succumb to them. Instead, he consistently sought to live and write out of the paradoxical experience of Christian faith that offered hope for the homecoming while maintaining the condition of strangerhood. This tension that is fundamental to the "unhomely" grammar of Christian faith points the way toward creating community in a world that is not yet home.

In the pages that follow I will explore the peculiar ability Christian faith imparts to those who take up its discipline with any degree of seriousness to live in particular locations as strangers. I will focus on the grammar of Christian faith that makes one a stranger and at the same time creates a commonality of its own. The spirituality of strangerhood has the capacity for making connections symbolically and materially where the basis for such does not yet exist. Over the generations, human beings have typically taken materially given categories (such as land, tribe, "race," gender, class, language, or culture) to be the basis for community. But the universalizing message of the Christian gospel contains within it a criticism of the adequacy of any such given, calling its hearers to a commonality that is yet to be created. If there is any power to the Christian gospel, it is this power that makes women and men who are strangers to one another neighbors. At the same time, such a practice must make one a stranger to the idolatries of land, tribe, "race," gender, class, language, or culture, thereby making women and men who are neighbors to one another strangers. This might well be the fundamental paradox of

Christian life and faith, if not a compelling reason for the church—any church—being and becoming a "frustrated fellowship."[4]

I am using the phrase "the grammar of Christian faith" here in place of the more common terms "doctrine" or "dogma" to point toward its regulating function in Christian practice. Early Christian tradition spoke of doctrine as the *regula fidei,* or "rule of faith." Doctrines or dogmas were not isolated truths merely to be believed for their own sake, but provided the guidelines for Christian liturgy and life, or devotion and practice. I understand them to be the same today. The Christian story of God with us in Jesus Christ, of God's Spirit poured out upon all flesh, continues to provide options for behaving and ways of speaking about the world that empower one to live and act differently than one otherwise would. True doctrine changes the world, it doesn't merely reflect it. It authorizes among those who are Christians a different way of speaking about the way the world is. Christian doctrines or grammatical rules of faith authorize what Gayatri Chakravorty Spivak often refers to as *catachreses,* words or phrases used out of context, or that have no literal referent. Christians speak in meaningful ways about a world that is not this world, about a world that does not (yet) exist.

This is a crucial point to make: the doctrine of Christian strangerhood is not one of Christian homelessness. Christians are not people without a home, without a referent. They are people whose home is "over Jordan," or "on the other side." It is a "holy" home (in the sense of holy meaning "other," that which is set apart). The same Jesus who is remembered to have said that "the Son of Man has nowhere to lay his head" is also remembered as telling his disciples "I go to prepare a place for you."[5] Homi K. Bhabha calls this sense of "beyond" an "estranging sense of the re-location of the home and the world—the unhomeliness—that is the condition of extra-territorial and cross-cultural initiations."

> To be unhomed is not to be homeless, nor can the "un-homely" be easily accommodated in that familiar divi-sion of social life into private and public spheres. . . . If, for Freud, the *unheimlich* is "the name for everything that ought to have remained . . . secret and hidden but has come to light," then Hannah Arendt's description of the public and private realms is a profoundly unhomely one: "it is the distinction between things that should be hidden and things that should be shown," she writes, which through their inversion in the modern age "dis-covers how rich and manifold the hidden can be under conditions of intimacy."[6]

I don't expect that either Homi Bhabha or Hannah Arendt would recognize their concept of extraterritorial and cross-cultural initiations, or an inverted public-private distinction, in this Christian dogmatic form. But that is precisely what I am proposing James Washington under-stood about the spiritual praxis of Christian faith, specifi-cally as it was given historical form in African American life. The liturgy of African American worship was a vehicle for psychic and material deliverance, Washington argued. This is no reduction of religion to its utilitarian purposes. Rather, it is the ground out of which authentic community emerged beyond the ordeal of day-to-day existence within the throes of a modern racist regime. African Americans experienced in worship a world that was more real than the present worlds of slavery, Jim and Jane Crow oppression, or late capitalist commodification.[7]

This, then, is the heart of the paradox of unhomeliness and strangerhood: Christians are people who share a common reference that is not a part of their given context, that is extraterritorial and thus cross-cultural. It is precisely this inverted, translocational experience that joins them together as their common bond, their *koinonia*. Strangers (*paroikoi*) to one another in the world of human habitations (the *oikoumene*), they become neighbors and members of one another in the new household (*oikos*) of God. The grammar of this faith is to be found in historical relationships, as any grammar is found in its practice. Another way of saying this is that Christian faith is always incarnational and relational. The Word becomes flesh and dwells among us, in Jesus Christ and in his continuous presence in the community of disciples who seek to live with him. The church itself is the body of Christ, an unhomely household that inverts its dimensions and transcends its contexts.

The paradox of Christians being strangers and neighbors continuously leads us to the location of Christian community, the church. The church is a community that lives by the catechetical grammar of Christian faith. Its self-understanding is found in the doctrine that it is a household belonging to a different order. As a community, the church is always on location. Like a stranger however, the church always lives with reference to something that is beyond its location. Here the incarnational lens that the Christian tradition offers us can provide a necessary corrective to the tendency in modern thinking to fracture the one beam of light into its various constituent parts on a spectrum, then try to illuminate a topic with one color at a time. The modernist sensibility has separated word and flesh, theology and ethics, theory and praxis, so that we

cannot often see that Christian community *is* the herme-
neutic of the gospel, and that the grammar of Christian
faith is embedded *in* Christian life and community. The
word becomes flesh in praxis, although its referent always
remains beyond it. "Christ has died. Christ has risen.
Christ will come again," one says in the Christian eucharistic liturgy.

How does it work? How does the catechresis of Christian corporate life finally bring about material connection
and not just ideological or idealistic connection? How can
we speak of the church as community when there is no material basis for such given to us in the material forces. These
fences after all are the embodied material referents by
which collective identities of family, neighborhood, and
country are derived. Without some such means of material
mediation for community life, the church can never be
more than a voluntary association or a public arena—a
marketplace for exchanging religious ideas, perhaps, but
still not a home. If the church is only a symbol system,
then it faces the danger that confronts all symbol systems
in a late capitalist environment, that of commodification.
Words like "church" and "community" are then very
much in danger of becoming emptied of their material
meaning (however much it might be a material future to
which they are pointing), making them little more than
slogans in a modern "church growth" advertising campaign.

Raising the question of the material value of language
and ideas is intentionally pointing us in the direction of
Karl Marx, that philosopher of material relations and modern prophet of social change.[8] More than a century ago
Marx foresaw the total commodification of all arenas of social life as the end of capitalism, and sought to sound the

alarm about it. One of his key philosophical concepts in his later works was that of value, which he understood to be the mediating factor in material economic relations. Toward the end of his 1857–58 notebooks, *Grundrisse*, Marx provided a brief analysis of the value of a commodity which, he said, actually combines two different forms under one appearance. The first is that of "use value," the value an object has in meeting the satisfaction of human need. For Marx, use value is a presupposition for commodification, and it is a constant. "Wheat, e.g., possesses the same use value, whether cultivated by slaves, serfs or free labourers. It would not lose its value if it fell from the sky like snow."[9] For wheat to become a commodity, however, it must have added to it "exchange value," the value an object has within the marketplace. This latter form represents the transformation of objects of human production, and ultimately human beings themselves, into commodities. The process of commodification is for Marx the fundamental idolatry of the capitalist era.

Then almost in passing, Marx points out that the line between use value and exchange value is also the boundary by which we define community: "Exchange begins not between the individuals within a community, but rather at the point where the communities end—at their boundary, at the point of contact between different communities."[10] The relationship of exchange, Marx is arguing, provides the edge of community. Beyond it is the market, an externalizing relationship, the beginning of strangers. Those whose relationship is one of use value, or for whom use is the common value, are community. The more common term for this is sharing, *koinonia* in the language of the New Testament. Marx uses the example of children and parents to make his point: when children pay their parents room and board, it is no longer a household or family. So also the traditional "spontaneous economy of societies" was the basis for community. In a society in which the market becomes totalized and totalizing, community is impossible, and all are strangers to one another.

It is at this point that the economy of Christian faith is most radical, and most subversive, however. In the same letter to Diognetus quoted at the beginning of this essay, the author writes that Christians share their table, but not their beds. Simply put, sharing a table subverts the economy that makes us strangers to one another, in the first century or the twenty-first. J. B. Metz has argued that the Christian eucharist holds a "dangerous memory" that is politically subversive.[11] Here it can be argued that the Christian eucharist is equally subversive of material economic relations of exchange. It offers grace that is free. "Come, buy wine and milk without money and without price" proclaims the prophet Isaiah (55:1b). God's grace is not found in a relationship of exchange—this is why we are no longer strangers to God. The eucharist communicates and mediates this grace that is free, and in doing so it creates and consecrates community. Its materiality—bread that has been formed by human labor from the wheat Marx referred to, wine that has come from the vine of human labor as well—is continuous with the materiality of the historical person of Jesus and the material relations of the church. As such, the eucharist cannot be only a "spiritual" meal and leave untouched the material relations of those who gather for it. The sacramental economy does not leave us strangers to one another, even as it makes us strangers to a world that only knows external relations of exchange.

Toward the end of the second century of the common era, Irenaeus, bishop of Lyons, wrote:

And just as a cutting from the vine planted in the ground
fructifies in its season, or as a corn of wheat falling into
the earth and becoming decomposed, rises with mani-
fold increase by the Spirit of God, who contains all
things, then, through the wisdom of God, serves for the
use of men [and women], and having received the Word
of God, becomes the eucharist, which is the body and
blood of Christ; so also our bodies, being nourished by
it, and deposited in the earth, and suffering decomposi-
tion there, shall rise at their appointed time, the Word of
God granting them resurrection to the glory of God.[12]

Those who have passed on in their material bodies hence
are not disconnected through the eucharistic economy in-
fused by the word who is Jesus Christ. Even the dead are
not to be strangers. James Washington often reminded
those who would listen to him that the people we study in
our history classes were once flesh and blood, and that our
study of them must ultimately come to grips with this fundamental datum of their humanity. When we do so, he argued, then we will have come to grips with the fundamental datum of our own humanity, a humbling proposition of
which he never ceased to remind us.

SEEMING SILENCE AND
AFRICAN AMERICAN CULTURE
*Interruption as a Metaphor of Transformation
in the Religious Historiography of
James Melvin Washington*

Lucas Wilson

Your archives reveal past prayers that engaged the creeping
issues of theodicy that threaten to sour our covenant with
Thee. Only you know how many of your black children are
angry with you. Like Cain, it is easier to kill Abel than to
admit anger with our Divine Parent. Some of us scream,
Why do you favor Abel, especially when Abel has more than
he needs? Your silence pains us. Our souls demand justice.

—JAMES MELVIN WASHINGTON

IN the introductory essay to his anthology of conversations with God,[1] James Washington tells the story of
Praying Jacob, a black slave in the state of Maryland. Praying Jacob was so-called because he had an unbending rule
to pray, at an appointed hour, three times a day. As remembered by Greenburg Offley, a black Methodist minister,
Praying Jacob would interrupt his slave labors, no matter
what his work was or where he might be, to kneel down and
pray. He risked whipping and even death at the hands of
his slavemaster to pray to the master of his soul. Even with
a loaded gun placed against his head, Praying Jacob insisted on his human, God-given need to pray, knowing that
by claiming it *as a right* he was performing in order to

transform, in bodily and spiritual form, the central contradiction of those who would sanction black slavery in the
name of a Christian God. In exercising his right to pray,
Praying Jacob also participated in the constitution of a
"heavenly discourse"—a language of becoming in the
world through conversation with God about the world
within which he and other African slaves who found themselves in a situation of absurd suffering could work out
their salvation, and could also rationalize, reinscribe, and
endure the horrifying practices following from that central contradiction.[2]

The story of Praying Jacob serves as a point of departure for my reflections on the work of James Melvin Washington. As an archivist, teacher, preacher, scholar, pastor,
mentor, and friend, his work—the sum of all these practices and more—offers insight and encouragement to those
of us who, faithfully and ruthlessly, strive as people of God
to be effective cultural workers, organizers, and freedom
fighters in the United States. I offer these reflections as a
way to celebrate and commemorate his life. This occasion
is also an attempt to begin to come to terms with his legacy
as that legacy informs my life and work. By taking a broad
view of one man's study of a group's historical and cultural
experience, my reflections are an attempt to take an even
larger view of a large man, to view him at his "soaring"
best. It is how I knew him, and how I remember him.

James Washington situated his work (including the notion of "interruption" that I want to examine in this essay)
within the discourse of "the black story," by which he
meant the many and myriad, conflicting and contingent,
rule- and structure-governed utterances, texts, and stories
of striving and world-making, often through religious language, of African American people and their allies. "The

black story," for James Washington, is a discursive formation, constituted by sacred and mundane elements, whose
narrative quality consists of (1) its emphasis on the cen-
trality of undying, doubt-filled faith in imminent divine
revelation and ultimate salvation and, (2) the practical
mandate of commitment to the ebb-and-flow but never-
ending struggle against all forms of oppression. Discourses
of "the black story," past and present, stand as consequence and critique of blasphemous American white racist
discourses during slavery and since.[3]

In his scholarship James Washington sought to recover
the politics of black religious movements. His work, including a dissertation which became the seminal history of
the black baptist convention, ranged from the study of organized movements for freedom during slavery to an analysis of the tradition of symbolic politics of Black Christendom witnessed in the 1984 presidential campaign of
Jesse Jackson. Throughout, he explored the nature and implications of the claim that black culture and experience
are part of God's new revelation to the world. He was concerned to demonstrate that God's revelation, and the manner in which divine revelation became known to us, was in
the form of an "interruption." African American history
and culture, in Washington's conception of "the black
story," was a series of *divine revelations experienced as interruptions*. He regarded African American religious and
political culture, then, as a culture of crisis and critique.[4]

Jacob, a slave, praying.

It is a powerful metaphor: a black slave who insistently
prays to a Christian God. The sacred moment of prayer is
forcibly and inextricably tangled with the mundanity of
being black and therefore legal chattel. What possibilities

does this metaphor produce as we try to imagine a cultural politics in it? To progressive Christian folk, what postures does this metaphor commend? To answer this question, it is necessary first to clarify a few terms.

A metaphor is a linguistic process in which attributes of one object are transferred to another object. A metaphor can be thought of as a term that transfers meaning from the literal to the figurative realm of language. But a metaphor of transformation makes a greater demand on theoretical work. Perhaps it is more than a play of words through the use of imagination. Stuart Hall explains how some metaphors may serve to model or represent a *process of social and cultural change*. Metaphors of transformation, as he refers to them, embody the theoretical work of "thinking through" cultural critique, crisis, and change. They are culturally constructed conceptualizations of the radical imaginary that help us to think our way into and out of the ideological and material structures against which we struggle. Another feature of metaphors of transformation is that they appeal to us, in part, because they are capable of expressing in non-essentialist, partial ways the discursive limits within which we make and have our being.[5]

Hall argues that a metaphor of transformation must accomplish at least two tasks: First, it must provide a vision, a sense of what human experience would be like once the old worlds—the old social hierarchies, old standards and norms, old conditions of existence—have been "overthrown" and new meanings, new social relations, new cultural configurations have begun to emerge. Second, it must have analytic value. That is, metaphors of transformation "think" us, and in so doing, offer us insight into how we might "think" ourselves differently. The importance of this second task cannot be overstated. Hall writes:

> This question of how to "think," in a nonreductionist
> way, the relations between "the social" and "the sym-
> bolic," remains *the paradigm question* in cultural the-
> ory—at least in all those cultural theories (and theorists)
> which have not settled for an elegant but empty
> formalism.[6]

Reading the story of Praying Jacob as a metaphor, we see
that a transfer of meaning from the material (or social) to
the spiritual (or symbolic) realm takes place. In the process, the metaphor becomes a way to articulate real, material conditions (chattel slavery in the United States) and
their multiple, overdetermined symbolic effects.

What meanings are transferred? A first and crucial fact
about Praying Jacob is that he was a black slave. Praying Jacob understood that the legal, social, and economic order
into which he was born was profoundly shaped by this fundamental absurdity: the white men who preached the universality of humankind with the Judeo-Christian Bible in
one hand, deployed often brutal technologies of profit,
control, and death in the other. Having the status of "ani-
mate chattel" was the overwhelming meaning of Praying
Jacob's life in this formulation.

This "mundane" detail of "the black story" launches us
into the more expansive "mundane story" of captivity and
removal—forced migration—from Africa to the so-called
New World, the sunup to sundown regiment of black slave
labor in the American South, the failed promise of two attempts at "Reconstruction," and the abandonment of the
black poor we now face. But that's not all there is to this
"black story." James Washington was among those who
emphasized the moments of agency in black cultural expression. In response to his enslavement, Praying Jacob
articulated a politics of the body in which his humanity

was not guaranteed by his slavemaster's version of who he was. Rather, Praying Jacob subverted the institutionalized hegemony of that version of who he was bodily—a slave— with another version of who he was spiritually—a child of God who stood in judgment against the institution of slavery. Put differently, the mundane story is overdetermined by a sacred story. In the sacred story, Praying Jacob's evolving sense of self, the ground upon which he negotiates the worth and meaning of his existence, takes place "outside" bodily enslavement, and thereby constitutes a critique of slavery. That is, his praxis of prayer was a spiritual enactment of the slaves' critique of the dehumanizing effects of slavery. This spiritual (or symbolic) enactment had material consequences.

My focus in this essay is on the work of interruption. Movement from one realm to another, the transfer of meaning from the social to the symbolic realm, occurs through an interruption. Praying Jacob interrupts his work to kneel and pray. The mundane story is interrupted by the sacred story. In James Washington's religious historiography of African Americans, this interruption produces a transformation. In interrupting his work to pray "no matter what or where," Praying Jacob acheived a "work slowdown," but more important, he, along with other slaves, participated in the development of the chattel church, an organic, autonomous cultural and political institution against which the dominion of his slavemaster, ultimately, could not prevail. The formation of a religious social movement was a material consequence of Praying Jacob's interruption. Organized against black slavery, institutions of black worship became primary sites for debating and celebrating the politics of revolution and resistance. The sacred story, the symbolic politics of black spirituality, was the space in which slaves knew, understood, and strategized "freedom."

Like many black slaves who converted to evangelistic or pietistic Christianity, Praying Jacob believed that spiritual bondage was a greater affliction than material bondage. In fact, many historians of slave religion conclude that slaves believed that freedom from spiritual bondage was a precondition of, and would lead to, freedom from material bondage. But more than that, Washington insisted that the moral critique brought to bear upon slavery through the "chattel church" was part of a critical intelligence that in turn became part of the evolving social identity of slaves and continues in African American culture up to the present. He concludes that these earnest-hearted servants of God, rather than submit to despair, hatred, and anger, built a social movement that, to this day, is still the largest independent black organization in the United States.[7]

It is fascinating and instructive to reflect on the ruggedness of faith, the willed citizenship in the "not yet," that is so powerfully on display in the sacred story of the Christian faith of black slaves. By inhabiting the "not," their humanity was worked out. This subversive "move" is evidence that, from the beginning, they were active agents who understood and opposed the injustices imposed upon them, and their days were days of resistance as well as (and again, sometimes in the form of) days of accommodation. Always, especially during the lonely hours of God's seeming silence, they believed that the Judeo-Christian God was a liberator. With that faith, black slaves who became Christians engaged the struggle on two fronts (the symbolic and the social), enduring the myriad "frustrations" of slave/black Christian fellowship.[8]

The complex relationship between sacred and mundane stories is not a novel way of reading African American religious and cultural history. As my retelling suggests, the tension between sacred and mundane stories has more often than not implied a smooth, *un*interrupted unity between them, a shifting back and forth in dialogic and dialectical fashion between this-world and "other"-world understandings of black predicaments. Most observers interpret black religious practices as an index of the degree of their material impoverishment and powerlessness. Many argue that vital spiritual resources have been an absolute necessity, a constant presence, for Africans throughout the diaspora whose histories and cultures were displaced by "the Middle Passage."

A growing number of black religious scholars, by contrast, grant that the relationship between mundane and sacred stories is complex, but insist that it is also overdetermined. They insist that the two stories form a complex unity, and that in their relations to each other they simultaneously and mutually effect one another. The mundane conditions of existence of black slaves, for example, cannot be understood by simply reducing the sacred story—the deeply held, mythic understandings of self and world—to those mundane details. The sacred story is not a sophisticated, ideological reflection or redescription of the mundane in which African Americans are admired for how they suffer, righteously and with dignity. Conversely, it would be a mistake to interpret the mundane details of African American slave (or other) experience as part of the "outward manifestation" or the "mirror image" of some inward, divine or natural design for the people of the world, and in this case African Americans are seen to be tragic victims of the divine or natural order. Instead, sacred and mundane stories are of a piece with one another, and together they are involved in the making of a dynamic, syncretic culture of purpose and promise. Together they produce a vision that stands as a critique and alternative to images of dignified sufferers of tragic victims.

Theophus Smith, for example, reads the history of African American spiritual traditions through the simultaneity of sacred and mundane stories. For him, the vision contained in "the black story" is appropriately framed as a quest, not for freedom, but for community:

> One way to cast the black story renders it the pilgrimage of a people toward freedom. That construction is readily understandable and has its merits, but it can also absorb the pre-slavery background of African traditions into a liberal democratic ethos peculiar to the American experience (and forecasts the foreseeable future in such terms exclusively). A more inclusive and arguably indigenous approach frames the story as a quest for transcendant community or *communitas*. As a framework that can include the imperatives of freedom and justice, the quest for transcendance in community is also more continuous with a West African ethos that values as preeminent a harmony of one's tribe with the spirit world of gods and ancestors.[9]

Smith's understanding of the relation between sacred and mundane stories is informed by Stephen Crites's classic analysis. The quest for transcendant community, a more overarching description that decenters the goal of "freedom" at the core of most narratives of the experience of black slavery in the Americas, speaks not only to the ongoing struggle against racism, but also to the theoretical and existential need to envision a world before (and after) race and racism. The sacred story is, in a way, home, although for some, home bears the pleasures and trappings of paradise. In transcendance, one is able to discover the limits of mundane, corporeal experience, even in those instances where more secular forms of myth suffice for God-talk.

Like Smith, Crites also defends analyses of depth, arguing that there are "fundamental narrative forms," sacred stories, within which our sense of self and world is created. Sacred stories, he says:

> orient the life of people through time, their life-time, their individual and corporate experience and their sense of style, to the great powers that establish the reality of their world. Sacred stories are anonymous and communal, yet they are not perceived as conscious fictions. Sacred stories, and the symbolic worlds they project, are not like monuments that men behold, but like dwelling-places. People live in them. [T]hey are not directly told [and] a culture seems rather to be the telling than the teller of these stories.[10]

He adds,

> Sacred stories, too, are subject to change, but not by conscious reflection. People do not sit down on a cool afternoon and think themselves up a sacred story. They awaken to a sacred story, and their most significant mundane stories are told in the effort, never fully successful, to articulate it. For the sacred story does not transpire within a conscious world. It forms the very consciousness that projects a total world horizon, and therefore informs the intentions by which actions are projected into that world.[11]

Following Smith and Crites, we may conclude that a group's sacred story is embedded in the discursive universe of the mundane story. In this sense, the sacred story "thinks" a people. The mundane story, however, is the actual story told (of, for instance, African people's survival in the West over four centuries of struggle) to convey "objectified images" in the phenomenological order.

> The stories of an age or a culture take place within its
> world. Only in that sense are they necessarily mundane.
> Here, in some world of consciousness, we find stories
> composed as works of art as well as the much more mod-
> est narrative communications that pass between people
> in explaining where they have been, why things are as
> they are, and so on. Set within a world of consciousness,
> the mundane stories are also among the most important
> means by which people articulate and clarify their sense
> of that world.[12]

Sacred and mundane stories overdetermine one another. The distinction between them suggests that they
cannot be separated neatly. Just as Praying Jacob's religion, as described in his religious practices, cannot be ab-
stracted from the fundamental fact of his being a slave, it
would make little sense to try to understand "slave culture," or "the economics and politics of slavery," without
taking seriously their heavenly discourses. The metaphor
of Praying Jacob, in other words, provides a context in
which we can interpret a black cultural politics. But to do
so requires that we abandon the essentialist methodologies
of reductionism (the mundane story is, in its essence, a
watered-down form of the sacred story), and the scientistic
impulse to privilege the "master sense" of vision (the sacred story is "subjective knowledge" because it cannot be
measured, tested, or otherwise empirically verified, as if all
scientifically accepted truths met, and passed, this standard). Doing this allows us to probe the work—the transformative work—of interruption.

Interruption is the relation of linkage between sacred
and mundane stories. It expresses how sacred stories are
grounded in the mundane (in history), and how the mundane gives poetic expression to unutterable sacred stories.
Or, it could be said that interruption is the mediating form,

the primary character of linkage between sacred and mundane stories. In either formulation, interruption as a metaphor of transformation in James Washington's work poses a challenge to social scientists—economists, in particular—who take the question of culture seriously in their analytic work. Indeed, a great difficulty in completing this essay has been to think my way across the chasm that stands between an economics literature that posits some form of African American culture, and African American cultural studies texts that attempt to take seriously the role of the economic. I believe James Washington's use of interruption as a relation of linkage between the social (mundane) and the symbolic (sacred) represents a major challenge to both literatures, but it is a challenge that, if rigorously engaged, will prove productive.

What are some of the moments of interruption in James Washington's work? The first interruption is one that accounts for his distinguished career as a scholar and teacher of modern and American church history at Union Theological Seminary, New York City: "I have been pursuing a vocation in the field of church history since April 4, 1968." The assassination of Martin Luther King Jr.

> raised serious intellectual and existential questions for me. These questions of evil (both human and possibly divine) pricked my nascent intellectual gifts. . . . It was then that I came to the belief that intellectual modernism and King's notion of "the crisis of the American conscience" were inextricably related. Indeed, I could not understand how academics could claim that their work should not and could not be a reflection of their own existential pilgrimage.[13]

From the beginning his scholarly project was linked in a deliberate and conscious way to the ground, to the social formation, or "the times," that provided the conditions of possibility for him. His project, working in the academy to reproduce himself in the form of black Ph.D.s and working as a research historian to uncover "the black story," was a response to historical events that had a profound impact on him. Who he was, what his project was, was decidedly *not* a private choice made after a calculation of the benefits and costs of scholarly life in ivory towers here in the United States. King's death "interrupted" an early career in church ministry, prompting him to spend the rest of his life trying to understand how his ancestors responded to similar experiences of loss; how the "modern intellect" accounted for the gripping problem of theodicy; how human social movements for good, for freedom, were again and again frustrated by catastrophic human evil.

In his inaugural lecture (October 1987) he wondered, What did it mean for *him* to succeed Robert T. Handy, or to join the ranks of Tillich, Neibuhr and Shinn, and Martin, Brown, and Trible, and Cone, West, and Forbes, at this seminary? Unlikely it was, he thought, for someone who started out on Isabella Circle in the Jim Crow segregated world of Knoxville, Tennessee, to end up a trustee of knowledge at one of the leading seminaries in the country. Not that he thought himself unworthy. Hardly. But what "interruptions"—here again—were necessary for such an appointment to occur?

In exploring the "grace" moment of interruptions, he wrestled with the *intellectual* significance of his appointment. Perhaps nowhere did he more emphatically argue his case for the intellectual significance of his appointment, or for the intellectual significance of "the black story," than in his analysis of a crisis in American church historiography. In "Craven Images," he deconstructs the received tradition of writing American church history, the primary commitments revealing whose stories count; the importance of the question of who writes, and when, and where; the culturally specific values affirmed and rejected as primitive. His deconstructive work is an interruption—it is a way of staking out a place, his place and the place of "the black story"—in the field of American church historiography. The analysis he offers in that essay is an example of historical and theoretical work as struggle, as a dogged attempt to grapple with questions of representation, self-representation, institutional change, and ongoing epistemological crises concerning the production and status of historical knowledge.

The work of interruption involves struggling with the historical and theoretical traditions that inform our work as a way of recognizing the influential power of that tradition, and also as a way of recognizing its limits. Washington believed that the time was ripe for the work he did. He was encouraged in his sense of an epistemological and historiographical "rupture" by Sydney Ahlstrom's prediction in 1972 that "the basic paradigm for a renovation of American church history is the black religious experience," and by George Hunston Williams' prophecy in 1951 that "[t]he comprehensive, momentous, historical interpretation of the nature and destiny of American Christianity" might be written by "an American Negro historian of the Church." These comments from his intellectual mentors (Ahlstrom was his dissertation supervisor) stood as challenges he tried to meet in his life.[14]

As a historian of modern and American church history who specialized in African American spirituality, James Washington attempted to meet these challenges by doing extensive work in collecting and cataloguing sermons, songs, prayers, diaries, birth and death certificates, and church records of countless African American ministers, congregants, and churches. He recognized that the entire field of American church history would be transformed by the iterative interruptions of scholarly treatments of black sacred and mundane stories of deliverance and salvation.

In pursuit of his project, his sympathy and his empathy were with testimonies like the one found in the story of Praying Jacob. His sympathy and empathy were demonstrably not with those who rationalized the technologies of human suffering developed and used in the name of profits, progress, or punishment. He regarded the testimonies of black folk as expressions of a "reigning assumption" concerning spirituality and nurturance in African American Christian community: "God is a living, personal presence that is insinuated at all times and in all circumstances." He believed that the sacred and mundane stories together formed a complex, overdetermined unity. As one, they constituted a way of narrating "the black story." And with both aspects of experience in focus, he saw that the historical experience of struggle against racism, against white supremacy, was always, at least in part, a spiritual struggle, and that practitioners like Praying Jacob used prayer and other forms of worship to impeach human sin. Mundane logics of race could be, and were, interrupted by the spiritual (symbolic) practices of African Americans.

In this cultural politics, the dispensation of the body was not the final verdict. The silence of God in the midst of the unrelieved human suffering of African Americans was only seeming. That is what Praying Jacob understood. It is what James Washington understood as well. Perhaps it is why Cornel West described him as "a prisoner of hope in these desperate times." When God seems silent, as in the profound silence of Golgotha heard most audibly by Jesus himself; when the cause and end of faith seems to have disappeared, as in the gathering of one million black men in the nation's capital to ask God why they (we) suffer so, or in the forsaken pits of the Nazi Holocaust; when there is no "interruption," actual or imminent, as in the lonely hour of the last instance when the oppressed desperately seek for relief from their misery; when the hope of our race seems more like the desperate dream of a powerless and unlucky people; when sorrow seems the only song—then, James Washington believed, we are in the moment when, in the words of Barbara Brown Taylor, we are most able to recognize that

> [o]nly an idol always answers. The God who keeps silence, even when God's own flesh and blood is begging for a word, is the God beyond anyone's control. An answer will come, but not until the silence is complete. And even then, the answer will be given in silence. With the cross and the empty tomb, God has provided us with two events that defy all our efforts to domesticate them. Before them, and before the God who is present in them, our most eloquent words turn to dust.[15]

It is no small achievement to recognize, and then to compellingly argue, that an essential element of "the black story," part of that story's critical politics, was and remains its sacred story, its claim that racism is a form of religious idolatry. And once it is granted that the practices of producing or opposing race and racism are, from the perspective of "the black story," spiritual practices, it becomes necessary to ask, as James Washington did, "What is this thing called *race* good for from a spiritual perspective?" How does it work for us, and against us? What is it about race that we want to do away with? What about it do we cling to, fearing that we cannot live without it? How are racism's benefactors to be convinced of their own idolatrousness, their own blasphemy? Or, in the secular language of our therapeutic age, which he sometimes used, How are racism's benefactors to be persuaded that they are ill, crippled by a social disease they experience as a perverse form of pleasure? These and other questions concerning the changing same of "race in America" were questions it became possible to ask—in this way, in this place, with these implications for scholarly and political work—only at a particular time in history, only under specific historical conditions. These were the conditions under which he labored, and the conditions that gave form and content to the quality of hope he sustained to the end of his life:

> I want to question, though, the way we're suggesting a decline in spirituality. I don't see decline. I see change. But it's been so rapid that we have not been able to index it. I think that people believe in something. It's very difficult to sustain life without some belief or some faith. It's very hard. Maybe you believe in the needle, and you move from one shot to another. But why? Are you trying to anesthetize your pain? What's the nature of your pain? You find out what people believe in, what their faith is, then you'll know what their spiritual practice is. If you keep doing that sort of spiritual archeology, you can get at the taproot of what is troubling someone. [P]eople have not changed all that radically—they're just serving new gods. If we work hard enough on ourselves, we can constitute the beginnings of what King called "the beloved community." And I think that in the end that's what we're after. But there's a whole lot of work to be done.[16]

"SOME FOLKS GET HAPPY AND SOME FOLKS DON'T"

Diversity, Community, and African American Christian Spirituality

Cheryl Townsend Gilkes

THE CHURCH was crowded that Sunday and I had not yet reached the age where any of the sermons made sense. I was also so little that I had to peek around the pew and look down the aisle in order to see my father's friend, Deacon Singleton. He was my favorite deacon because he would start singing songs that the congregants joined in and sang with no books, thumping their feet with no piano or organ. For some reason, I loved those songs. It was one of those Sundays when all the signs of a really good service were present. Deacon Singleton had raised a hymn and then Mrs. Rippey had sung my favorite gospel song, "Since I Met Jesus." As the Gospel Chorus members walked back to their seats, Mrs. Sinclair began to fling her arms outward while crying repeatedly, "Thank You, Jesus!"

While the rest of the congregation waited patiently for her to finish, I whispered to my mother, "Mommy, what is that lady doing?" My mother replied quickly, hoping to keep me quiet, "She's shouting." I then continued, "Why is she shouting?" My mother then spoke soothingly and with authority, "Because she feels the Spirit." Realizing that Jesus was in the congregation in what I thought of as His invisible Casper-the-friendly-ghost form, I then asked, probably to my mother's consternation at this point, "Do *you* feel the Spirit?" As she leaned over to tell me, "Yes," I noticed a tear moving down her cheek. I then followed through with the pursuit of logical conclusions, peculiar to four- and five-year-olds: "Then why aren't you shouting?" I do not remember her exact words, but when she was finished, I knew that everybody did not feel the Spirit the same way. Later on I would hear gospel singers sing what my mother had taught, what Paul preached, and what most black folks believed: that when "some folks get happy," others do not, that "there [really] are diversities of gifts, but the same Spirit [a]nd . . . differences of administration, but the same Lord."[1]

Years later I learned that Deacon Singleton's songs were called "common meters" or "Dr. Watts" songs.[2] I learned that some churches were shouting churches and some churches were not. Indeed, the congregation of my childhood was officially pronounced "dead" by many gospel singers who sang at our annual choir festivals. As I scrunched down in the corner of the choir room while they changed into their robes, I listened to their complaints. I was engaged in a form of pediatric ethnographic fieldwork and I learned that my church was "dead" and visiting gospel singers had to "work too hard" when they sang. Inevitably, I also learned that the Gospel Chorus sat with the congregation rather than in the choir loft, not because the piano was there, but because the chorus' status was lower than the Senior Choir who sang the anthems and wore hats with their robes. I later learned that gospel music came to my church and many other Baptist churches on the heels of a protracted cultural struggle.[3] A church at any given moment represents an outcome of contested culture.

Mercifully, little children are fairly well protected from the cultural struggles and conflicts that swirl around them. I was more fortunate than most. My parents always answered my questions about church and religion. Junior Choir and Junior Usher Board memberships meant that I visited the full range of black churches on Sunday afternoons. Summers took me away to the churches of my grandparents and my aunts. I was exposed to lots of churches, where I learned to accept a wide range of behavior from people moved by the Spirit. My grandfather, a general elder and pastor in a denomination of the Sanctified Church,[4] occasionally came out of his pulpit and holy danced at the end of his sermons. Since I could always see Grandad, I was more interested in watching the tambourine, guitar, drums, and saxophone that we did not have at my church even though we sang the same songs. Grandad was awfully quiet at home and usually fasted on Wednesdays, the day he wrote his sermons. I know because he once tried to convince me to join him in fasting; I insisted that he go to the kitchen and fix me a full breakfast, bacon, eggs, grits—the works. I carefully followed him around the kitchen watching his every move; he never even licked his fingers! I was duly impressed. At my aunt's church, women actually got up out of their seats, got out into the aisles, and shouted louder than Mrs. Sinclair—and I couldn't understand what they were saying! Throughout my childhood I moved back and forth through a multiplicity of religious experiences that shaped my spirituality and collectively constituted the Black Church.

The Black Church is a diverse world of denominational

and cultural constituencies whose histories are shaped in part by a variety of doctrinal, social, and political conflicts. These constituencies share a commitment to a set of practices and beliefs that distinctively emphasize the role of the Holy Spirit in corporate worship and in the organization of individual belief and personal spiritual life. Thus black Christian spirituality—the spirituality of the Black Church or African American Christianity—is rooted and grounded in a religion of the Spirit distinct from, but not unrelated to, African religions and African-derived religions in the New World that practice and emphasize what Joseph Murphy called "working the Spirit" or, more precisely, the S/spirit(s).[5]

Spirituality is a concept that is always in process and its definition at any moment must be grounded in the beliefs and practices of particular communities. African American Christians enthusiastically embraced the biblical dictum in which Jesus promised the presence of His Spirit among the smallest of gatherings, saying, "Where two or three are gathered together in my name, there am I in the midst of them."[6] That belief and the different approaches to its practice have fostered an amazing diversity of churches and religious bodies from mighty mega-churches to humble house churches, and a wide variety of convocational, nondenominational, and popular spiritualities. Black Christian spirituality is embedded in a religion of the Spirit that depends on adherents' honoring the authority of their own and others' personal experiences and fostering an ethic of comfort with diverse expressions of their interaction with the Spirit. Such diversity was a fact of life in the earliest moments of African American history and defined the context in which Africans and their descendants constructed culture and religion in the New World. African traditional religions and Islam provided the foundation for African American Christianity; that Christianity, W. E. B. Du Bois later argued, was a "gift" and a significant cultural force for the entire society. The diverse expressions of African American Christian spirituality facilitated the reconnection, therapy, healing, and reconciliation needed in the lives of black people as they resisted the destructive forces of racial oppression. The religion of the Spirit enables people surviving in a context of constant assault and crisis to remember, reweave, and reorganize meaningful cultural fragments.

Spirituality reveals the connection between a person and a community. While there is no one definition of spirituality, there tends to be some agreement that the religious motivations, experiences, organizations, and beliefs of individuals form a special mix that constitutes and defines a community's spirituality. The most underappreciated and undertheorized dimension of spirituality in the black experience is this ethic of comfort with spiritual diversity. This ethic depends upon the authority of personal experience. People cooperate to produce the sacred and this cooperation defines the best and most effective traditions of black spirituality.

African Americans cooperate in this production through the stories they embed in their prayers, testimonies, and songs, as well as in their sermons.[7] In order for the connection between the personal and the communal to bear fruit, each person's story has to be respected and honored. One learns early, growing up in black churches and listening to people's stories, that everybody's behavior eventually makes sense. The kinship that emerges among the diverse segments of the Black Church comes through the multiple stories that emerge in every single discourse in the churches. Those stories are connected not only through the real and fictive kinships that make it possible to imagine and constitute community, but through time they also constitute a history.

In the Beginning: The African Foundations of Diversity

Perhaps more than any other American religious tradition, African American Christianity or the Black Church emerged from the negotiation of diversity.[8] Negotiation is a process, according to sociologist Anselm Strauss, through which people produce a coordinated social order, "a negotiated order," through activities aimed at achieving the paramount goal of an organization. People agree, disagree, create, uncreate, make rules, break rules, develop interpretations, discard those interpretations, and so on in order to work together in spite of the competing interests, unequal resources, and different commitments they possess. Negotiation is a form of construction work, *social* construction work, that produces a cultural space where people can survive and solve problems. The "negotiated" social order is dynamic and under constant revision from within as people move in and out, and as the problems a group or organization confronts change and new constituencies emerge. The African American experience is just such a cultural space, and the Black Church a negotiated order that engenders and nurtures spirituality.

The beginnings of African American culture are defined by the negotiation of diversity that occurred among

Africans whose consciousness and experience confronted the shock and trauma of life in the New World.[9] A learning process took place that had already begun in the Old World; trade, war, domestic slavery, migrations, and resettlements generated a very practical approach to interaction among traditional African religions. Mintz and Price argue that the multiple religious specialists in West and Central African cultures who "owned" ritual knowledge through kinship and cult groups created a condition that

> encouraged experimentation with, and adoption of, new techniques and practices from neighboring peoples; we suspect that most West and Central African religions were relatively permeable to foreign influences and tended to be "additive" rather than "exclusive" in their orientation toward other cultures.[10]

The enslaved Africans' diverse ethnicities, languages, and religious traditions represented a starting point, not a stumbling block, for building black cultures throughout the Americas. The diverse ritual responses to problems in living and life represented the beginnings of African American culture in the New World.

The construction of culture is about the creation, accumulation, and passing on of a group's knowledge—the strategies, techniques, symbols, artifacts, and systems of meaning that foster survival. Both physical and psychic survival are involved. Psychic survival is at the core of human spirituality. Religious ritual was necessary for psychic survival and, as Mintz and Price point out, ritual exchange between members of diverse African societies made such survival possible:

> We can probably date the beginnings of any new African-American religion from the moment that one person in need received ritual assistance from another who belonged to a different cultural group. Once such

people had "exchanged" ritual assistance in this fashion, there would already exist a micro-community with a nascent religion that was, in a real sense its own.[11]

Throughout the Americas, these ritual exchanges grew into a wide variety of African-derived religions, which creatively incorporated new "foreign" material.

A unifying theme in these religions has been a process that Richard Murphy calls "working the Spirit."[12] In some way every African-derived religion in the New World underscores the working of the "S/spirit(s)" in the lifeways and persons of the believers.[13] In the varieties of these religions, worshippers express with their voices and their bodies the diverse administrations of the S/spirit(s) during the ritual experience.

Spirituality usually involves imagining the divine with reference to the character of the community. For feminist spirituality groups, that often means imagining the divine as feminine or appropriating goddess traditions.[14] Traditional African religions, particularly Yoruba or Yoruba-related religions, imagined the divine in multiple terms.[15] These multiple images addressed a wide variety of problems and situations of human life. As various religious systems interacted, connected, and reinvented themselves in the New World, the old gods sometimes developed syncretic and symbiotic relationships with Catholic Christianity and Native American cultures, or these old gods became metaphors of connection with the biblical imagination in Protestant Christianity.[16] According to Zora Neale Hurston, African American folklore sometimes interpreted Moses in terms of Fon/Yoruba images of divine power, especially images of Moses's rod/serpent.[17] The traditional praise song "He's a Battle Axe"[18] harkens not only to the vision of the prophet Jeremiah but also to the

African orisha Ogun—the spirit of iron and, therefore, truth.[19]

The biblical imagination of the Black Church underscored and highlighted the image of God as Spirit. Not only did African Americans embrace a biblical promise of that Spirit's presence "wherever" and whenever, but they also took seriously Jesus' insistence that "God is a Spirit: and they that worship him must worship him in spirit and in truth."[20] The emphasis on the person of the Spirit incorporates and embraces multiple images of God. Jesus is central to faith but at the same time Jesus is a matrix for imagining. God is also, as the songs eventually declare, Ezekiel's wheel a-turning, Moses's bush a-burning, Solomon's Rose of Sharon, a shelter in the time of storm, a doctor, a lawyer, a friend, a mother to the motherless, a father to the fatherless, and a walking cane to glory. God can be, do, and move in infinite personages, remains all-powerful and all-knowing, and is fully committed to be present "wherever two or three touch and agree."

Finally, the social organization of West and Central African societies added to the foundations of religion and culture in the New World. The elaborate kinship networks of these societies permitted people to be kin to one another in a variety of ways. Women particularly were caught in a web of kinship affiliations and ritual obligations involving their own and their children's kinship systems. By just simply being their children's primary agents of socialization women became authorities on spiritual diversity within their own families.[21] Women's spiritual importance was magnified through their memberships and leadership in autonomous women's societies and religious groups. Traditions of multiple memberships in title societies and religious organizations (cult groups) further reinforced the internal diversity of African societies and the multiple ways an individual could be a member and therefore be accountable to multiple constituencies within a community. Margaret Washington Creel and others point to the continuities between African secret societies and the secret and benevolent societies their descendants formed before slavery ended.[22]

When there are multiple ways of belonging to a community, people are not bound to one particular setting in order to actualize their spirituality. As religious actors, people seek and create multiple stages for doing spirituality, multiple places to be spiritual. If the Baptist Church of one's childhood does not seem to approve of shouting and speaking in tongues, one can hold her peace until her cousin's holiness church has the annual revival and go "around the corner" to move beyond being simply "saved" and become "sanctified, Holy Ghost filled, and fire baptized."[23] Then, as one family of sisters in my church did, one can return to the home church and be a presence, a knowledgeable presence, prepared to help the church when it finally catches fire. The plurality of places to be spiritual also means that organizations that are not churches may presume that being spiritual is the normal order of business; meetings of sororities, fraternities, Pullman car porters, Prince Hall Masons, literary clubs, and voter registration organizers all begin with prayer. Leaders are expected to be spiritual and to include the spiritual in their agenda.

African American Spirituality as Cultural Force

When Du Bois described "Negro religion" in the United States, he called African American Christianity "the Gift of the Spirit."[24] His analysis of African American spirituality as "a gift" characterized black religion as a cultural force shaping the entire society. In 1903, he pointed out that

> the religious growth of millions of men [and women],
> even though they be slaves, cannot be without potent in-
> fluence upon their contemporaries. The Methodists and
> Baptists of America owe much of their condition to the
> silent but potent influence of their millions of Negro con-
> verts. . . . It is thus clear that the study of Negro religion
> is not only a vital part of the history of the Negro in Amer-
> ica, but no uninteresting part of American history.[25]

While Du Bois was highly critical of the conflict that characterized the Black Church, he later expanded his analysis, arguing that "the gift of the Spirit" represented "the peculiar spiritual quality which the Negro has injected into American life and civilization."[26]

In an unusual configuration of biographical elements, Du Bois "discovered" African American spirituality during his undergraduate years at Fisk University while teaching at a rural school during the summer. Du Bois had grown up in western Massachusetts and was accustomed to the religious rectitude of New England Puritans, a tradition that was "quiet and subdued." He also grew up hearing his grandmother singing a song that reflected the family's African origins. Attending a revival in the rural Southern community prompted the reflections on black religion that integrated the African and the American in his thinking. Du Bois identified three basic elements of "the faith of the fathers" (really the faith of the mothers and the fathers), which he called the preacher, the music, and the frenzy. The principal voices of the black religious experience were those who were empowered by the community to speak for and to the community in its ritual moments and in other moments of crisis. The black preacher represented the indigenous and organic leaders who organized and mobilized.

While the focus has traditionally been on the black male pastor, observations on church life and the Civil Rights Movement demonstrate that such an understanding of leadership is too narrow. Long before Du Bois observed that rural revival, the voices of women, speaking for and to the community, were present. Women preachers, worship leaders, and exhorters were very much a part of the slave community. Free women preachers, most famously Zilpha Elaw, were occasionally granted safe conduct through the slave states of the South in order to preach.[27] Both men and women served as the big voices necessary to maintain a lifeline of vision for African Americans.

Du Bois described this leadership as inextricably linked with the voices and the actions of the people in their most spiritually expressive and collective moments: "the frenzy" and "the music." This organic connection through corporate spirituality was the source of the leader's effectiveness. The preacher chanting his sermon evoked and provoked diversities of gifts and differences of administrations in the people. The people sang their songs and shouted their praise in response to or in control of the preacher, as they defined and revised the situation in their own souls. Through this process of being spiritual black people built a precious component into the culture—a *spirit* of democracy that served to reconstruct and make America.[28]

(RE)MEMBERING CULTURE:
BLACK SPIRITUALITY IN CRISIS

At no time in their sojourn in the New World have black people been free from the constraints of economic exploitation, political exclusion, and cultural humiliation. Every diverse expression of spirituality has been shaped in a context of oppression and crisis. That is not to say that African American spirituality is simply reactive. To engage African American spirituality is to engage a system of conflict, fragmentation, reconnection, and reintegration—a system straining toward unity through dynamic interaction among multiple constituencies in a context of diversity and of varieties of religious experience, belief, action, and feeling within and beyond ritual settings. The diverse ways in which human beings insist on simply being human in inhumane circumstances have implications for current trends in religious practice. Spirituality defines and constitutes humanity.

An ethic of comfort with diversity is still a fact of African American spirituality. African American religious history is filled with splits and schisms, but it is also filled with sustained kinships, reconciliations, interconnections, reconnections, and convocational alliances. This ethic challenges black people to take a creative, constructionist approach to doctrine and dogma in order to build community, periodically criticizing the irrationality of religious boundaries that foment conflict. Black folklore and litanies from the preaching tradition raise questions about religious divisions among Christians that are not easily answered. In his 1903 essay on religion, Du Bois was concerned about the increasing class differentiation that he observed.[29] Yet he saw potential for revolution and challenge in the church that others did not see. Du Bois described a cooperative spirituality in which the preacher was inseparable from the community and the community was proactive in its demands on its leadership.

The genius of African American Christian spirituality is its ability to transcend boundaries of class, color, ethnicity, and geographic origin; such trancendence was hardwired into the faith during slavery. This ethic of comfort with diversity, however, also served as a vehicle for carrying the ideas of hope and love into the Civil Rights Movement and for empowering black people to name and confront the evils that oppressed them. The religion of the Spirit generates an assertive response to psychic and material deprivations. The Spirit that empowered church mothers in the Sanctified Church to step forward boldly, lay hands on suffering people, and pronounce them healed or cleansed is the same Spirit that permits individuals who have been knocked down, deprived, and humiliated to rise up, restored, renewed, and revived—healed and re-membered.

LETTER TO JAMES

A Conversation on Archeology and Soul

E. Lee Hancock

Dear Jim,

I am on St. Catherines Island, one of the "golden isles" situated off the coast of Georgia, a crew member on an archeological expedition sponsored by the American Museum of Natural History. St. Catherines is a little-known island; however, its history, like the concentric growth rings of ancient trees, tells a story about various conquests of native and subjugated peoples. Now it stands wild and undomesticated,[1] as if the lush and demanding environment has decreed that the voices of human history are those to be heard, rather than the cacophony of the present. But these voices are heard, and their stories told in relic and ruin. The stones do indeed cry out. In this place, you are indeed on my mind.

Archeologists have located seven-thousand-year-old burial mounds here; the Indians who inhabited this place are only known by the name Guale, the name given to them by the conquering Spanish. Although this group of native people spoke *Muskhogean,*[2] no one knows what they called themselves. It is thought that these Native Americans were probably Creek Indians, but what is left of their history is present only in their artifacts of daily life. What was once their garbage is sacred to the archeologists, who tenderly sift through soil and shell to discover and caress a tiny bead.

This place and my experience here hold so much that was central to your life. So many of its multiple meanings were embodied in your ministry: early American history, the voices of subjugated people, the struggle for survival and meaning, the sublime art of story telling and the numinosity of the environment. As one with an unquenchable thirst for knowledge and a passion for American history, I knew you'd love this story.

The Franciscan mission of Santa Catalina de Guale was established on the island less than seventy-five years after Columbus first set foot in the New World. It was Georgia's oldest known European settlement and part of the extensive mission system established by the Spaniards in the Eastern United States.[3] By 1680, the mission Santa Catalina de Guale had been deserted. In response to attacks by the British, the small Spanish group fled southward in a slow retreat to St. Augustine. Abandoning the mission signaled the beginning of the demise of Spanish power in the southeast. In a few decades, the mission was lost, covered by fierce and sturdy vegetation. The history of the vast Spanish presence was lost as well.[4] What remained was the story as told by the Franciscans and the story of the Guale Indians captured in the dirt.

The priests had come to convert the Indians; building their mission in a spot on the island so that any traveler on the intercoastal waterways would see a beacon witnessing to the presence of the Church of Christ.[5] The priests did effect religious conversion, but it was also their aim to "raise the aborigines from their primitive state, often characterized by a very low degree of culture, to that of civilized and responsible citizens of the Spanish Empire."[6] I wonder what was the gospel story that the priests, Miguel and Antonio, told the Guale Indians, and what story did they think they were supposed to tell? Was it a story of obedience and power, of cultural oppression masked as truth? Unfortunately, the story of oppression is a wearisome, shameful, and repetitive story, told as testimony to your legacy. The priests lived in the convento, said Mass, and regulated the life of the Indian people, until they began to undertake their mission of transmuting the Guale into Spaniards by requiring fundamental changes in their social structure. Apparently, the imposition of religious ritual was insufficient to the task of cultural oppression and hegemony. "Simultaneous polygamy was to be replaced by Christian monogamy."[7] In 1597, the Guale Indians staged the earliest documented anticolonialist rebellion in North America.[8] The chief came to the priests and told them to get their affairs in order, because they were to be killed in a few days. The chief made good on his promise: the priests were chopped into bits and their body parts thrown into a grave outside the church. The bells of the mission tower were then hacked to pieces in an apparent effort to stop the constant and incessant sound that regulated their lives. Michel Foucault understood and articulated well how the lives of the oppressed are policed through the internalization of the gaze;[9] in this instance, it was manifested in the ringing of the mission bell. Apparently, when a mission bell was damaged, the priest would not receive his pension until he had accounted for all of its pieces. Each bell was named and baptized, an extraordinary irony in a place where so many were stripped of the right to name themselves. If religion is indeed the community presenting itself to itself,[10] then the Natives must have decided that what they saw reflected back to them was a stunted and demented sight. Needless to say, the imprint of oppression and cultural imperialism is not easily erased.

Eventually the mission was rebuilt, and although the fighting between the British and Spanish continued for many years, the Spaniards withdrew from St. Catherines. Button Gwinnett, one of the signers of the Declaration of Independence, purchased the island with the hope of growing corn, indigo, and rice, because a vast network of plantations had begun to prosper in the area. During the antebellum era, however, much of the land on St. Catherines was cleared to produce cotton.[11]

The history of this island is a microcosm of oppression in American history. Just as archeologists analyze the levels of soil at various depths, each stratum producing new information, each layer of history adds a new dimension to the story of oppression. The "big house" and the exterior of a cotton gin remain, as do the "tabbies," slave quarters made of shell and lime, where once daub and wattle formed the structures of hearth and protection. Trenches are still visible that once inscribed the parameters of the fields. Majestic old trees dot the landscape; they are both harrowing and haunting, for they marked the place where slaves could find some shade in the great open fields of agricultural enterprise and human degradation. Sorrow emanates from these immense live oaks; resurrection ferns grow up on their great arms while Spanish moss drapes and hangs from their branches, a visual allusion to the willows that weep. The fields are no longer open or cultivated; they are covered by second-growth forest, but the noble "slave trees" still stand, far larger and more grand than anything in their proximity. The beauty and grandeur of the magnificent live oaks suggests that they functioned as the tree of life in those days when slaves worked the fields, the axis mundi for those who sought respite during the grueling days of relentless labor.

In the exquisite and extraordinary introduction to your book *Conversations with God,* you tell the story of Praying Jacob, a slave in the State of Maryland[12] who would not, under any circumstances, relinquish his time for prayer during days of back-breaking labor. Daily he risked his life, if not the cruel wrath of his master. Looking at these trees, I imagine that he must have fallen to his knees underneath a great tree of life, its body etched with the outlines of grief, its wind song, a cry. Faith was his axis mundi, signifying, like the great trees, the center of his universe, giving strength and meaning. The enduring question you pondered in this essay is the central problematic of prayer. "Why," you ask, "do people who suffer, continue to believe in a God who supposedly has the power to prevent and alleviate suffering?"[13] The problem of suffering is the great koan at the heart of Christianity, but it implies a conception of power, undoubtedly faithful to the Exodus story but a vision of power nevertheless, that projects an inscrutable and inconsistent God, who hears the cries of the faithful but chooses, even in the face of great suffering, to observe but not alter the external circumstances of individual lives. This is the great theological conundrum of the twentieth century, inscribed on each emaciated but faithful body in the Holocaust. Is it struggling to offer the critique that we conceive of power only in human terms or that our infantile selves know no patience and only demand change? Immediately and on our own terms? I am sobered by the ending of the Book of Job.

Does the brilliance of the African American spiritual experience of which you write lie in the realization that deliverance does not begin with transforming external factors and events, but with the transformation of the *experience* of suffering, which in turn empowers? We cry to God for deliverance, yet deliverance begins in the relation, the internal transformation, which bleeds forth into external reality. Isn't that the substance of the fierce faith of Mrs. Grady, whom you eulogize in this essay? It is this faith that flies in the face of our spiritually nascent selves who demand rescue when we have no faith, fearful that something might be asked of us. When divine power does not accrue to us, then do we abandon the discipline of prayer? Prayer externalizes the inner relation; faith, the "evidence of things unseen," the conviction of the present nearness of another reality, transforms the impersonal into the personal. In the existential crisis of life, shaped by meaninglessness and absurdity, the taste of intimacy in a world hostile and alienating at best, cruel and destructive at worst, is life giving, an anchor, a piece of bread, an embrace.

Undoubtedly, it is the intimacy of and the contact with another dimension that transforms lives. It is the contact with, *not* the belief in, the power of another reality that is transforming. This is the difference between theology and spirituality. If faith is the "evidence of things unseen," that is to say, the experience of the divine and not the intellectual assent to and belief in the divine, then faith transforms the impersonal into the personal. The great enigma of human life is this: Is the universe personal? Is there a vast fierce tenderness that counts the hairs on our heads and numbers our days? Is the existential angst of life manufactured from the meaninglessness of human existence, or is it a product of our fear of an impersonal cosmos? As I walk under the stars and hear the ancient voices of St. Catherines, this question is at hand; the radiance of the stars bring it so close that you catch your breath. Stargazing is, as you point out, a spiritual exercise, a cleansing, restorative, and healing exercise, exorcising the demons of dullness, predictability, and hubris. Not only does it engage our imagination, but it provides us with a perspective by which we might measure the significance of our insignificant lives. Some Native American traditions hold a belief in the Great Star Nation from which we all come and to which we will all return. This creates an intimate relationship with the cosmos; our home is in the stars. The distance between us stirs our longings, and gives shape to our yearning to become, and return to our celestial home. It excites us, reminding us that we are given a light, we are meant to shine. Our "transporting to the stars" provides evidence of a personal cosmos; we are not only welcomed, but invited by the sheer energy and magnetism of the stars to engage our wonder, our delight, our imagination. It exists for us.

Here on St. Catherines, it is the landscape that tells the greatest story. The landscape is in the foreground of every experience. Landscape usually functions as background, stale to our numbed eyes. On this island, the landscape is both background and foreground; its magnificence is awful, awe-filled, awe-filling. It is a land virtually barren of the construction of human culture, where creation, not the artifacts of human civilization, stand at the foreground of experience. The night is asphalt black; there are no paved roads, highways, or telephone lines. There is nothing to light up the celestial heavens but the stars themselves. They do not compete for attention; they capture and enfold you with their light, which is distinctly palpable. They reach out for you, inviting relationship. The trees sing a haunting song as the wind blows through them. They moan and whisper and cry, they carry the voices and history of times past, an unsettling and constant reminder of stories lost and lives stolen. In their indistinct but audible language, the songs of the trees are the sounds of this uninhabited island, punctuated only by the voices of multitudinous birds. Theirs is a song in a minor key, a song of the failure of the human project to reap little more than human misery. It is as if the landscape stands in harsh judgment of what is human. The environment declares, "Be still and know that I am God." On Easter morning, I conducted a service at the site of the old Spanish mission and read from your anthology. We read prayers of slaves, prayers against racism. We read prayers from Indian nations, in some small attempt to honor the voices of those silenced, voices at times heard only by God, which were raised with the conviction and in the assurance that *someone, something* was listening, that there was and is a presence, a beingness that receives the cries of the faithful, the moans and sighs too deep for words of those who not only believe in but *know* the experience of an intimate relation with the cosmos.

But what does this *mean* in a nihilistic world? Does it offer anything? If relation is the essence of life, then this truth extends to the seen and the unseen alike. The Celtic scholar John O'Donohue offers the wisdom of the Celts as an antidote to the dualism and materialism, the principalities and powers of this age. It seems as if we are all reaching back to the wisdom of the ancestors to free us from the captivity of this age to the harsh dualisms that only engender and reinforce alienation. John O'Donohue states that in the Celtic world, there was no separation between inner and outer, between above and below, between the seen and unseen worlds.[14] Not only is this idea intellectually appealing, soothing our human (rational?) need for consistency, it heals our alienation and fragmentation. Yet it also carries a mandate for righteousness.

Righteousness has always been a deeply troubling word for me. It never seemed to fit the lexicon of Protestant hegemony; in that context it was only a sign of trouble. "Righteousness" uttered in that context implied a manipulation of power for personal gain, for agendas or moral prescriptions which would establish a social or spiritual hierarchy. What does "righteousness" mean for a middle-class white women with roots in the soil of Southern terrorism, inhaling the night air and hearing the voices and cries of the past through the trees? To say that the cosmos is personal does not mean that it is individualistic; rather, the I/Thou relation extends throughout creation.[15] In the beginning was the relation. As a sometimes good if sporadic Calvinist, I do believe that the psychologists are right, that the work of relationship is repair.[16] In this truth I can situate righteousness as the work of repair in demanding liberation from the social amnesia of my people, who claim no moral or spiritual inheritance from the sins of our fathers and mothers. In the true Calvinist tradition, ours is the prayer of confession, the cry for forgiveness. For those of us situated as oppressor, to resist cultural hegemony is to repair the past and the present. So we pray also to repair, which is a primary act of healing. Righteousness declares that the work of resistance is to counter this amnesia by being knowledgeable of, and accounting for, the history of slavery, of African America, of native peoples, of the colonized Guale Indians of St. Catherines island, of the silent and suppressed voices from then and now. You remind us that "the sin is to do nothing to resist and change the conditions that encourage us to remain either ignorant or forgetful. Resistance however, requires the prophetic insight and guts to examine the infrastructure of out own souls in search of the contours of the social malignancy of racism."[17] This is the work of righteousness that challenges the evil of pseudo-speciation[18] by claiming, simply, that we are all children of God, brothers and sisters to one another. No genetic, biological, or ontological hierarchies are allowed in the kingdom.

You are the materially absent but wholly present signifier in this wild and undomesticated place. I know that the stars speak your name, and in our stargazing, you are gazing back. From the continuum of time and eternity, spirit and material, seen and unseen, with the raucous laughter of angels gustily singing "How Firm a Foundation," you will continue to be present to us, enrich and inform our lives, gently and stubbornly challenge us from your deep well of irony, knowledge of human nature, and unswerving commitment to righteous healing. Rest well, my dear friend.

> Your sister,
> Lee
> St. Catherines Island
> Easter, 1998

BENEDICTION

Cornel West

> No intellectual or historical mapping can fully locate the
> Cross in the landscape of concept and of sensibility as our
> century closes. For participants in an overwhelming secular,
> technologically oriented society, this location is a "black
> hole" left by mythologies and unreason out of the past. For
> the majority, one suspects, of "practising" Christians—and
> what does "practising" entail in this context?—the Crucifix-
> ion remains an unexamined inheritance, a symbolic marker
> of familiar but vestigial recognitions. This marker is revered
> and involved in conventional idiom and gestures. Its concrete
> status, the enormity of suffering and injustice it incarnates,
> would appear to have faded from felt immediacy. How many
> educated men or women now hear Pascal's cry that humanity
> must not sleep because Christ hangs on his Cross till the end
> of the world?   —GEORGE STEINER

JAMES MELVIN WASHINGTON was first and
foremost a black intellectual Christian obsessed with
the meaning of the Cross in his time and in his life. He was
the existential giant and spiritual genius among us for
forty-nine short years because he unrelentingly brought his
largeness of mind, heart, and soul to bear on the profound
truth of evil in the human predicament. He not only
understood that a condition for truth is to allow suffering
to speak but also that the courage to hope is grounded in a
heartfelt grappling with the depths of suffering. In the
words of his beloved Paul Tillich, "there is no depth without the way to depth. Truth without the way to truth is
dead."

Jim was my best friend for twenty years. So I look at him

224

now through the lens of deep love and profound grief. As a product of Jim Crow Tennessee, he transcended American institutional terrorism by means of sheer intellectual power and spiritual grit. The life of the mind gave him some distance from the threat of social death and the Christian gospel provided him with a supportive armor against soul murder. His entry into the Christian ministry was his heroic effort to ward off the terrifying threats of nonbeing (of death, meaninglessness, and condemnation) and proclaim a support for the courage to hope.

In our daily lunch "seminars" at Riverside Church (often with James Forbes—now the distinguished Senior Minister), we intensely debated the meaning of the Cross—the whence and whither of evil, the sources of struggle against suffering, and the mysterious grounds of hope. We favored those existential thinkers of lived experience—those who thought and lived with passion and concern about death, despair, and injustice without the crutches of dogma or doctrine (Kierkegaard, Nietzsche, Barth, Tillich, Thurman, and others). And we always rooted our fierce exchanges in the concrete realities of everyday Black people dealing with the absurdities and indignities of American life.

My dear brother Washington was a "race man" in the best sense of that phrase. He was committed to the universality of human hope and possibility yet also preoccupied with the particularity of Black suffering. He was thoroughly convinced that the depths of the vicious legacy of white supremacy had been evaded by most American scholars and ignored by most modern intellectuals. And even the surfaces of this legacy have been misunderstood by many well-intentioned thinkers. His vocation as an interdisciplinary historian of American religion—encouraged by his Yale mentor Sidney Ahlstrom, the dean of American religious history—was to shatter the provincial frameworks and parochial paradigms that pushed Black doings and sufferings to the margins of serious historiographical inquiry.

His masterpiece, *Frustrated Fellowship: The Black Baptist Quest for Social Power*, was the first theoretical and historical treatment of the vast majority of Black Christians after slavery. His aim was not simply to tell a complex story about those left out by other historians but also to force all of us to rethink what we mean by modern and American conceptions of spirituality in light of the struggles of Black Baptists. His work required that we get beneath the surface of scholarship—its tendentious assumptions and mendacious presuppositions—and confront the depths of human responses to dark circumstances at the heart of America.

Washington was a unique historian owing to his philosophical bent. He focused primarily on how Black people constructed complex structures of meaning and feeling in white supremacist America. He was interested primarily in how African Americans became agents of their destiny in the form of creators of their sacred canopies. This focus and interest flowed from his own painful struggles with the meaning of the Cross in his life.

In this sense, his classic *Conversations with God: Two Centuries of Prayers by African Americans* was a heart-wrenching conversation with himself—as scholar, Christian, and preacher. Why hope in the face of overwhelming oppression? Why love in the face of violent institutional and individual hatred? Why struggle in the face of persistent defeat? He often talked and wrote about the sacrament of waiting—a major motif in his own prayers as well as the Black prayers he documented and interpreted. This view of writing as active engagement with the word (in stark contrast with the minimalist waiting in Beckett's *Waiting for Godot* or Eugene O'Neill's *The Iceman Cometh*) was a Christian form of being in the world. Its poles oscillated from the subversive joy experienced as Dionysian ecstasy of the Holy Spirit to the revolutionary patience enacted as eschatological anticipation—both in the context of black church revivals, liturgy, and beliefs. Yet are such Christian hope, joy, and struggle mere life illusions, life-lies, pipe dreams, or empty promises? Has not Black suffering, despair, and disappointment persisted in modernity? Is not post-Resurrection Black existence still more Cross-like than Easter-like? Do not Black people—indeed all people—live more intimately and honestly Good Friday or Holy Saturday than Easter Sunday? If so, why and whither Christian faith?

I call Washington a black intellectual Christian—rather than a Black Christian intellectual—because he always stressed "Christian" as a noun, not an adjective. Despite his profound love of Black people—and his incredible compassion of all persons in their individuality—and his inexhaustible (even legendary) intellectual quest for knowledge and wisdom, Washington remained a prisoner of Christian hope in the face of ground-shaking doubts and Job-like experiences. He still held on to the belief—as leap of faith not cognitive comprehension—that the meaning of the Cross yielded support for his blood-drenched hope that his love-inspired struggle was not in vain. Despite his well-grounded suspicions of the cheap grace often espoused by institutional Christianity—black and white, brown, yellow, and red—he banked his all on the costly grace enacted at Calvary. This grace simply says Yes in the face of a tear-soaked history of barbarity and No to every form of false security and frivolous idolatry. In this sense, Washington's heroic courage to hope was grounded in the groundless mystery of the Cross—a prophetic Christian witness to the absurd love of Jesus Christ in a fallen world that views such love as folly and appears to reduce such love to impotence. Washington understood this folly as Christian wisdom and lived this impotence as Christian hope. And some of us will never forget—and forever be empowered by—his tragicomic struggle, which embodied his Christian wisdom and hope. I believe I shall never see anyone like him again.

—Easter Sunday, 1999

NOTES

QUINTON HOSFORD DIXIE: *Introduction*

The quotation beginning this essay is from James M. Washington, "Craven Images: The Eiconics of Race in the Crisis of American Church Historiography," in Akintunde Akinade and Dale T. Irvin, eds., *The Agitated Mind of God: The Theology of Kosuke Koyama* (Maryknoll, N.Y.: Orbis Press, 1996), 139.

1 James M. Washington, ed., *A Testament of Hope: The Essential Writings of Martin Luther King, Jr.* (San Francisco: Harper and Row, 1986), xi.

2 Washington used this term to describe the way the previous generation of liberal church historians viewed black church history. He argued that they reduced the black religious experience to "an important addendum to a basically honest story." Washington, "Craven Images," 141.

3 See Washington, *A Testament of Hope*; and "The Crisis in the Sanctity of Conscience in American Jurisprudence," *DePaul Law Review* 42, no. 1 (1992): 11–60. Unfortunately, Dr. Washington died before he was able to begin the writing phase of his work on a religious history of the Civil Rights Movement. Nonetheless, his research will be available soon in the James Melvin Washington Papers at the Burke Library, Union Theological Seminary, New York City.

4 See for example, Washington, "The Origins of Black Evangelicalism and the Ethical Function of Evangelical Cosmology," *Union Seminary Quarterly Review* 32, no. 2 (1997): 104–16; *Frustrated Fellowship: The Black Baptist Quest for Social Power* (Macon, Ga.: Mercer University Press, 1986); and *Conversations with God: Two Centuries of Prayers by African Americans* (New York: HarperCollins, 1994).

5 Washington, "Craven Images," 136. See also Washington, "The Grace of Interruptions: Toward a New Vision of Christian History," *Union Seminary Quarterly Review*, 42, no. 4 (1988): 37–53.

DAVID D. DANIELS III: *"God's All in This Place"*

1 Lawrence Stone, *The Family, Sex and Marriage in England, 1500–*

1800 (New York: Harper and Row, 1970); Barbara Hanawalt, *The Ties That Bound: Peasant Families in Medieval England* (New York: Oxford University Press, 1989); Carmen Luke, *Pedagogy, Printing, and Protestantism: The Discourse on Childhood* (Albany: SUNY Press, 1989); Wolfgang Schivelbusch, *Taste of Paradise: A Social History of Spices, Stimulants and Intoxicants* (New York: Vintage Books, 1993); Suellen Hoy, *Chasing Dirt: The American Pursuit of Cleanliness.* (New York: Oxford University Press, 1995).

2 Emmanuel Levinas, *Outside the Subject* (Stanford: Stanford University Press, 1993), 19, 24-32, 55-59.

3 Armstead Robinson and Patricia Sullivan, eds., *New Directions in Civil Rights Studies* (Charlottesville: University of Virginia Press, 1991); Henry Hampton and Steve Fayer, *Voices of Freedom: An Oral History of the Civil Rights Movement from the 1950s through the 1980s* (New York: Bantam, 1990).

4 Andrew Young, *An Easy Burden: The Civil Rights Movement and the Transformation of America* (New York: HarperCollins, 1996), 185-241; Kay Mills, *This Little Light of Mine* (New York: Dutton, 1993); Keith D. Miller, *Voice of Deliverance: The Language of Martin Luther King, Jr. and Its Sources* (New York: Free Press, 1992), 153; Howell Raines, *My Soul Rested: Movement Days in the Deep South Remembered* (New York: Penguin Books, 1983).

5 Charles Payne, *I've Got the Light of Freedom: The Organizing Tradition and the Mississippi Freedom Struggle* (Berkeley: University of California Press, 1995), 413-42.

CHARLES H. LONG: *Passage and Prayer*

1 See Gerardus van der Leeuw, *Religion in Essence and Manifestation,* trans. J. E. Turner (London: George Allen and Unwin, 1937), part 2, section C, esp. 276, 280-81.

2 W. E. B. Du Bois, *Black Reconstruction in America* (New York: Russell and Russell, 1962), 727, emphasis added.

3 A sample of such works would include these titles: Vincent Harding, *There Is a River;* Eugene Genovese, *Roll, Jordan, Roll;* Thomas L. Webber, *Deep Like the Rivers;* Archie Smith, Jr., *Navigating the Deep River;* Sylvia Frey, *Water from the Rock;* and the first volume of Taylor Branch, *Parting the Waters,* a biography of Martin Luther King, Jr.

4 Fernand Braudel, *The Mediterranean and the Mediterranean World*

in the Age of Philip II, trans. Sian Reynolds. 2 vols. (New York: Harper and Row, 1972) is the modern comprehensive study of the power and impact of the Mediterranean Sea. Braudel shows how this inner sea structures human and ecological relations and takes on the primordial structure of time and reality.

5 The three volumes are *Structures of Everyday Life, The Perspective of the World*, and *The Wheels of Commerce* (New York: Harper and Row, 1986).

6 Volume 1: *Capitalistic Agriculture and the Origins of the European World-Economy in the Sixteenth Century*; (New York: Academic Press, 1974); Volume 2: *Mercantilism and the Consolidation of the European World Economy, 1600—1750*. (New York: Academic Press, 1980).

7 See Vincent Harding, *There Is a River: The Black Struggle for Freedom in America* (New York: Harcourt Brace Jovanovich, 1981), 25.

8 Mircea Eliade, *Patterns in Comparative Religion*, trans. Rosemary Sheed (London and New York: Sheed and Ward, 1958), 188.

9 William Pietz, "The Problem of the Fetish I," *RES* 9 (Spring 1985): 5–17; "The Problem of the Fetish II," *RES* 13 (Spring 1987): 22–44; "The Problem of the Fetish IIIa," *RES* 16 (Autumn 1988).

10 Pietz, "Fetish II," 23.

11 David Brion Davis, *The Problem of Slavery in the Age of Revolution 1770–1823* (Ithaca and London: Cornell University Press, 1975), 564.

ALBERT J. RABOTEAU: *"The Blood of the Martyrs Is the Seed of Faith"*

1 Peter Kalm, *Travels into North America*, 2nd ed., reprinted in *A General Collection of the Best and Most Interesting Voyages and Travels*, vol. 13, ed. John Pinkerton (London, 1812), 503.

2 Appeal to Governor Thomas Gage and the Massachusetts General Court, May 25, 1774, *Collection of the Massachusetts Historical Society*, 5th ser., 3 (1877): 432–33.

3 George P. Rawick, ed., *Arkansas Narratives*, vol. 8 of *The American Slave: A Composite Autobiography* (Westport, Conn.: Greenwood Press, 1972), part. 1, 35.

4 Benjamin Drew, *The Refugee: A North-Side View of Slavery* (Boston, 1856), 55.

5 Moses Grandy, *Narrative of the Life of Moses Grandy*, 2nd ed. (Boston, 1844), 35-36; Rawick, ed., *Mississippi Narratives*, vol. 7 of *The American Slave*, 24; Henry Bibb, *Narrative of the Life and Adventures of Henry Bibb* (New York, 1849), reprinted in *Puttin' On Ole Massa*, ed. Gilbert Osofsky (New York: Harper and Row, 1969), 123-25.

6 John Rippon, *The Baptist Annual Register, 1790-1793* (n.p.,n.d.), 340-41.

7 Drew, 270.

8 John Blassingame, ed. *Slave Testimony* (Baton Rouge: Louisiana State University Press, 1977), 276-78.

9 Rawick, ed., *Indiana Narratives*, vol. 6 of *The American Slave*, 158-59.

10 *American Missionary*, ser. 2, 11 (May 1862): 102.

11 Rawick, ed., *Florida Narratives*, vol. 17 of *The American Slave*, 166.

12 Clifton H. Johnson, ed. *God Struck Me Dead: Religious Conversion Experiences and Autobiographies of Ex-Slaves* (Philadelphia: Pilgrim Press, 1969), 76

13 Rawick, ed. *Texas Narratives*, vol. 4 of *The American Slave*, pt.1, 199.

14 David Macrae, *The Americans at Home*, 2 vols. (Edinburgh, 1870), 2: 102.

15 Johnson, ed., *God Struck Me Dead*, 74.

16 *American Missionary*, ser. 2, 6 (June 1862): 138.

17 Frederick Douglass, *The Life and Times of Frederick Douglass*, (rev. ed. 1892; London: Collier-Macmillan, 1962), 135.

18 Charles Carleton Coffin, *The Boys of '61; or Four Years of Fighting* (Boston, 1886), 415.

19 Barbara Leigh Smith Bodichon, diary entry of December 12, 1857, in *An American Diary, 1857-1858*, ed. Joseph W. Reed, Jr. (London: Routledge and Kegan Paul, 1972), 65.

20 See Johnson, ed. *God Struck Me Dead*, 23, 78.

21 William Grimes, *Life of William Grimes* (New Haven, Conn., 1855); reprinted in *Five Black Lives* (Middletown, Conn.: Wesleyan University Press, 1971), 198-99.

22 Drew, 181.

23 Howard Thurman, *With Hand and Heart: The Autobiography of Howard Thurman* (New York: Harcourt Brace Jovanovich, 1979), 134.

SANDY DWAYNE MARTIN: *Providence and the Black Christian Consensus*

1 Albert J. Raboteau, *A Fire in the Bones: Reflections on African-American Religious History* (Boston: Beacon Press, 1995), esp. pp. 17–36 and 37–56.

2 Albert Raboteau provides a good, overall description of African traditional religions and discusses the extent to which Africans in the Americas transferred their affiliations from the traditional religions to Christianity in his *Slave Religion: The "Invisible Institution" in the Antebellum South* (New York: Oxford University Press, 1978), esp. 3–92.

3 See Peter B. Clarke, *West Africa and Islam: A Study of Religious Development from the 8th to the 20th Century* (London: Edward Arnold, 1982). For an understanding of the context out of which Malcolm X operated for most of his public leadership years, see, e.g., Malcolm X, *The Autobiography of Malcolm X* (1964; New York: Ballantine, 1986); George Breitman, ed., *Malcolm X Speaks* (New York: Grove, 1965); and Claude Andrew Clegg III, *An Original Man: The Life and Times of Elijah Muhammad* (New York: St. Martin's Press, 1997).

4 See Allan D. Austin, *African Muslims in Antebellum America: Transatlantic Stories and Spiritual Struggles* (New York and London: Routledge, 1997), esp. chaps. 3–9, 51–186.

5 For a history of black Christianity, see Carter G. Woodson, *The History of the Negro Church*, 3rd ed. (Washington, D.C.: Associated Publishers, 1972); and the documentary collection of Milton C. Sernett, *Afro-American Religious History: A Documentary Witness* (Durham, N.C.: Duke University Press, 1985). For a historical sense of the spirituality of African Americans, see James Melvin Washington, *Conversations with God: Two Centuries of Prayers by African Americans* (New York: HarperCollins, 1994). For a more contemporary sociological/theological description of the independent black churches, see C. Eric Lincoln and Lawrence H. Mamiya, *The Black Church in the African American Experience* (Durham, N.C.: Duke University Press, 1990). Regarding the use of religious

imagery in formulating racial identity and purpose, see Wilson Jeremiah Moses, *Black Messiahs and Uncle Toms: Social and Literary Manipulations of a Religious Myth* (University Park: Pennsylvania State University Press, 1982).

6 St. Clair Drake, *The Redemption of Africa and Black Religion* (Chicago: Third World Press, 1970); Sylvia M. Jacobs, *Black Americans and the Missionary Movement in Africa* (Westport, Conn.: Greenwood Press, 1982); Sandy D. Martin, *Black Baptists and African Missions: The Origins of a Movement, 1880–1915* (Macon, Ga.: Mercer University Press, 1989).

7 See William J. Walls, *The African Methodist Episcopal Zion Church: Reality of the Black Church* (Charlotte, N. C.: AME Zion Publishing House, 1974), esp. 497–594. For an examination of Hood's thoughts relative to the black church and freedom, see James Walker Hood, *One Hundred Years of the African Methodist Episcopal Zion Church* (New York: A.M.E. Zion Book Concern, 1895); and Sandy Dwayne Martin, *For God and Race: The Religious and Political Leadership of AMEZ Bishop James Walker Hood* (Columbia, S. C.: University of South Carolina Press, forthcoming).

8 James Melvin Washington, *Frustrated Fellowship: The Black Baptist Quest for Social Power* (Macon, Ga.: Mercer University Press, 1986); and Gayraud Wilmore, *Black Religion and Black Radicalism: An Interpretation of the Religious History of the Afro-American People*, 2nd ed. (Maryknoll, N.Y.: Orbis Books, 1983).

9 Sterling Stuckey, ed., *The Ideological Origins of Black Nationalism* (Boston: Beacon Press, 1972), 30–117; and Sernett, ed., *Afro-American Religious History*, 88–99.

10 John Blassingame, *Slave Testimony: Two Centuries of Letters, Speeches, Interviews, and Autobiographies* (Baton Rouge: Louisiana State University Press, 1977); and Raboteau, *Slave Religion*.

11 See, e.g., Leon F. Litwack, *Been in the Storm So Long: The Aftermath of Slavery* (New York: Vintage Books, 1979), esp. 167–220.

12 See William R. Jones, *Is God a White Racist?* (Garden City, N.Y.: Doubleday/Anchor, 1973).

13 The Christianization of the black community manifested itself in the relationship between the press and the church. See, e.g., Hayward Farrar, *The Baltimore Afro-American, 1892–1950* (Westport, Conn.: Greenwood Press, 1998).

14 For an example of the proliferation of non-Protestant and non-

Christian religions during this era, see Arthur H. Fauset, *Black Gods of the Metropolis: Negro Religious Cults of the Urban North* (Philadelphia: University of Pennsylvania Press, 1971), and Aminah Beverly McCloud, *African American Islam* (New York: Routledge, 1995).

15 Randall K. Burkett, *Garveyism as a Religious Movement: The Institutionalization of a Black Civil Religion* (Metuchen, N.J.: Scarecrow Press, 1978).

16 Many scholars have written on Martin Luther King, Jr. Among the best overall examinations of King as both civil rights and religious leader are the works of Lewis V. Baldwin. See, e.g., his *There Is a Balm in Gilead: The Cultural Roots of Martin Luther King, Jr.* (Minneapolis: Fortress Press, 1991); and *To Make the Wounded Whole: The Cultural Legacy of Martin Luther King, Jr.* (Minneapolis: Fortress Press, 1992).

17 For a more comprehensive examination of African American Islam inclusive of but extending beyond the Nation of Islam and similar groups, see McCloud, *African American Islam*; and Steven Barboza, *American Jihad: Islam after Malcolm X* (New York: Doubleday, 1994).

18 For an example of the hostility that secular black nationalists often expressed toward the black minister and the black church, see James H. Cone, *My Soul Looks Back* (Nashville: Abingdon, 1982), esp. 54–57. It is not my intention, however, to claim that Cone would agree with my overall assessment of the Black Christian Consensus and the ultimate impact of secular black nationalism.

19 For a description of the nihilism current in much of contemporary black culture, see Cornel West, *Race Matters* (Boston: Beacon Press, 1993), 9–20. As with Cone, a disclaimer must be advanced. It is not my intention to claim that West agrees with the general thrust of this essay or the cause of this nihilism.

GENNA RAE MCNEIL: *Waymaking and Dimensions of Responsibility*

I gratefully acknowledge the very helpful critical comments of Quinton H. Dixie on earlier versions of this manuscript. This essay would not have been possible had I not been blessed to have innumerable conversations with my spiritual brother, James Melvin Washington, upon whose prayers I also depended and in whose memory this book has been written. This essay, however, is also dedicated prayerfully and lovingly to James Melvin's widow, Patricia, and daughter, Ayanna.

1 Philip Potter, *Life in All Its Fullness* (Grand Rapids, Mich.: Eerdmans, 1981), 1–2.

2 James Melvin Washington, *Frustrated Fellowship: The Black Baptist Quest for Social Power* (Macon, Ga.: Mercer University Press, 1986), xv.

3 James Melvin Washington, ed., *A Testament of Hope: The Essential Writings of Martin Luther King, Jr.* (San Francisco: Harper and Row, 1986), xii.

4 Michel de Certeau, *The Practice of Everyday Life* (Berkeley and Los Angeles: University of California Press, 1984), 178.

5 Ibid., 30.

6 John 14:6a (New International Version).

7 Howard Thurman, *Deep Is the Hunger* (1951; Richmond, Ind.: Friends United Press, 1973), 76. See also 73–75.

8 James Melvin Washington in *Restoring Hope*, ed. Cornel West and Kelvin Shawn Sealy (Boston: Beacon Press, 1997), 102.

9 Ibid., 99–102.

10 Washington, *Frustrated Fellowship*, xii.

11 The nomenclature for this periodization of African American history is based upon the work of Thomas Holt in "Whither Now and Why," in *The State of Afro-American History*, ed. Darlene Clark Hine (Baton Rouge: Louisiana State University Press, 1986), 2–3.

12 Reginald Hildebrand, *The Times Were Strange and Stirring* (Durham, N. C.: Duke University Press, 1995).

13 Washington in West and Sealey, eds., *Restoring Hope*, 110.

14 Ibid., 110.

15 Howard Thurman, *Jesus and the Disinherited* (Nashville: Abingdon Press, 1949), 109. When Thurman was writing, man was used in the nongendered sense, as *Mensch* is used in German, to include males and females.

16 Washington, *Conversations with God*, xxx.

17 See Dietrich Bonhoeffer, *The Cost of Discipleship* (reprint: New York: Macmillan, 1961), 47–48, 53.

18 See Samuel D. Proctor, "Finding Our Margin of Freedom" in *Ser-*

mons from the Black Pulpit, ed. Samuel D. Proctor and William D. Watley (Valley Forge, Penn.: Judson Press, 1984), 35–43. See also Howard Thurman, "The Growing Edge" in *The Growing Edge* (1956; Richmond, Ind.: Friends United Press, 1974), 179–80.

19 Samuel Proctor, "Finding Our Margin of Freedom," 38.

20 Thurman, *The Growing Edge*, 178.

21 Washington in West and Sealey, eds., *Restoring Hope*, 93.

22 James Melvin Washington, "Catching People," Sermon (text: Luke 5:11), Church of the Open Door, Brooklyn, N.Y., February 25, 1996.

23 Washington, "Catching People."

24 Washington in West and Sealey, eds., *Restoring Hope*, 93.

25 Undeniably, it is not a specific discourse on salvation, but rather the body of Washington's work, his ministry, his faith journey, and specific proclamations or pleas in sermons and prayers that sustain the argument posited in this essay. Privileged to be a spiritual sister and close confidant of James Washington, however, the author has relied upon a hollistic understanding of James Melvin Washington through his life and work, to begin a discussion of his views on salvation.

26 I would be remiss if I did not confess that the three aspects of salvation on which this essay focused were those particularly discussed by James Melvin in our professional as well as personal dialogues concerning faith journeys, worship, history, human relationships, and work. These understandings we also tested in myriad ways individually, but always offered them to God and each other in conversations that were punctuated with praise and constant queries in order to push the limits of the meaning of salvation in these "yet-to-be" United States.

27 Excerpt from James Melvin Washington, Pastoral Prayer, Church of the Open Door, Brooklyn, New York, March 2, 1997, 11 A.M. Worship Service (tape in possession of author).

JAMES H. CONE: *"Calling the Oppressors to Account"*

1 *The Works of Francis J. Grimke*, ed. C. G. Woodson (Washington D. C.: Associated Publishers, 1942), 1: 354.

2 James Baldwin, *The Fire Next Time* (New York: Dell, 1964), 46.

3 Martin Luther King, Jr., "Letter from Birmingham Jail" in his *Why We Can't Wait* (New York: Harper, 1963), 90–91.

4 *A Testament of Hope: The Essential Writings of Martin Luther King, Jr.*, ed. James M. Washington (San Francisco: Harper and Row, 1986), 233.

5 Ibid., 286.

6 Martin Luther King, Jr., "Thou Fool," Sermon, Mount Pisgah Baptist Church, Chicago, Ill., August 27, 1967.

7 Malcolm X, *The Autobiography of Malcolm X* (New York: Grove Press, 1965), 222.

8 W. E. B. Du Bois, *The Souls of Black Folk* (1903; Greenwich, Conn.: Fawcett, 1961), 23.

JUDITH WEISENFELD: *Difference as Evil*

This essay contains quotations from racist, anti-Semitic, and homophobic materials that some may find difficult to read. I remain committed to understanding, exploring, and exposing the intricacies of these discourses that pervade American cultures. Such analysis requires attention to the structures and mechanisms of these beliefs over against easy blanket judgments.

1 I would like to acknowledge and thank Timea Szell, Nancy Worman, and Quinton Dixie for helping me to think out and shape this piece.

2 To emphasize the constructedness of "race" is not to deny its salience in everyday life or its critical function in helping to forge community, identity, and cultures among oppressed peoples. Anthony Appiah writes, "These claims will, no doubt, seem outrageous to those who confuse the question of whether biological difference accounts for our differences with the question of whether biological similarity accounts for our similarities. Some of our similarities as human beings in these broadly cultural respects—the capacity to acquire human languages, for example, or, more specifically, the ability to smile—*are* to a significant degree biologically determined. We can study the biological basis of these cultural capacities and give biological explanations of our exercise of them. But if biological difference between human beings is unimportant in these explanations—and it is—then racial difference, as a species of biological difference, will not matter either. Anthony Appiah, "The Uncompleted Argument: Du Bois and the Illusion of Race," in *"Race," Writing, and Difference,* ed. Henry Louis Gates, Jr., (Chicago: University of Chicago Press, 1985).

3 David Hume, "Of National Characters," quoted in Henry Louis Gates, Jr., "Writing 'Race' and the Difference It Makes," in Gates, ed., *"Race," Writing, and Difference*, 10.

4 Charles Colcock Jones, *Religious Instruction of the Negroes in the United States* (Savannah, 1842), 104–5.

5 Josiah C. Nott, *Two Lectures on the Natural History of the Caucasian and Negro Races* (1844), in *The Ideology of Slavery*, ed. Drew Faust (Baton Rouge: Louisiana State University Press, 1981), 211.

6 Ibid 237–38, emphasis in the original. I do not mean to argue that these writers were connected to or dependent on one another's work in any way. This brief discussion is meant to define the shape of discourses about religion, race, and difference in the thought of many nineteenth-century white Americans.

7 I also want to note the work that scholars in women's history have done to emphasize the degree to which categories of race necessarily develop in relation to categories of gender and class. Thus, the meaning of "woman" becomes inflected given the particular racial and class location of the "woman" in question. See Evelyn Brooks Higginbotham, "African-American Women's History and the Metalanguage of Race," *Signs* 17 (Winter 1992): 251–74.

8 Toni Morrison, *Playing in the Dark: Whiteness and the Literary Imagination* (New York: Vintage Books, 1990), 6.

9 Jones, *Religious Instruction*, 105.

10 David A. Hollinger and Charles Copper, eds. *The American Intellectual Tradition*, vol. 1, *1630–1865* (New York: Oxford University Press, 1993), 15.

11 Josiah Strong, *Our Country*, ed. Jürgen Herbst (Cambridge: Belknap Press of Harvard University Press, 1963), 217–18.

12 Kingdom Identity Ministries [http://www.kingidentity.com].

13 Ibid.

14 James Theodore Holly, "The Divine Plan of Human Redemption in its Ethnological Development," *A.M.E. Church Review* (October 1884): 79.

15 Holly, 83.

16 Malcolm X, *The Autobiography of Malcolm X*, (New York: Ballantine Books, 1984), 165.

17 House of David [http://www.hodc.com].

18 Israeli Church of Universal Practical Knowledge [http://www.icupk.com/armageddon.htm].

19 James Baldwin, "An Open Letter to My Sister, Angela Davis," in Angela Y. Davis and Other Political Prisoners, *If They Come for Me in the Morning* (New York: Third Press, 1971), 14-15.

20 Kingdom Identity Ministries [http://www.kingidentity. com].

21 Transcript of White's statement in *The Wisconsin Light*, April 9-22 [http://www.wilight.com/page19.html]. White also told the legislature that God created races with different gifts—blacks for worship, whites for organization, Hispanics for family (meaning fecundity), Asians for scientific inventions.

22 Signed May 28, 1998, the order amends the already existing order by adding protection against discrimination in Federal employment on the basis of sexual orientation.

23 SBC Bulletin, Report of Committee on Resolutions, Southern Baptist Convention, June 9-11, 1998.

24 Anna Deavere Smith, writer and solo performer, *Fires in the Mirror: Crown Heights, Brooklyn, and Other Identities*, dir. George C. Wolfe. American Playhouse, Public Broadcasting System, April 28, 1993.

25 Anna Deavere Smith, writer and solo performer, *Fires in the Mirror: Crown Heights, Brooklyn, and Other Identities* (New York: Anchor-Doubleday, 1993), xxiii.

26 Smith, *Fires in the Mirror*, xxvii.

27 Ibid., xxvi-xxvii.

28 James Baldwin, *The Evidence of Things Not Seen* (New York: Henry Holt, 1995), 42-43.

29 Smith, *Fires in the Mirror*, 31.

WALTER E. FLUKER: *The Politics of Conversion and the Civilization of Friday*

1 Daniel Defoe, *Robinson Crusoe*, with illustrations by N. C. Wyeth (New York: Charles Scribner's Sons, 1920), 273.

2 "Dangerous memories fund a community's sense of dignity; they inspire and empower those who challenge oppression. Dangerous memories are a people's history of resistance and struggle, of dig-

nity and transcendence in the face of struggle." Shaton Welch, "The Beloved Community," *Spirituality Today*, "For the Trumpet Shall Sound: Protest, Prayer, and Prophecy" 40 (Winter 1988): 11–12; Johann Baptist Metz, *Faith in History and Society: Toward a Practical Fundamental Society* (New York: Seabury Press, 1980), 89. Nicolas Berdyaev, *Slavery and Freedom* (New York: Charles Scribner's Sons, 1944), 47.

Malcolm speaks of his personal quest for wholeness at a number of places in his autobiography. Malcolm X, *The Autobiography of Malcolm X* (New York: Grove Press, 1964, 1965), 187, 365, 368–69, 404, 408. David Garrow has maintained that the "kitchen vision" of January 27, 1956 in the early stages of the Montgomery boycott was the paradigmatic moment in King's spirituality. Martin Luther King, Jr., *Stride Toward Freedom* (New York: Harper and Row, 1958, 1964), 58–63. King, "Our God is Able," in *Strength to Love* (Philadelphia: Fortress Press, 1981), 113–14. David Garrow, *Bearing the Cross* (New York: William Morrow, 1986), 57–58; David Garrow, "Martin Luther King, Jr., and the Spirit of Leadership," in *We Shall Overcome: Martin Luther King, Jr., and the Black Freedom Struggle*, ed. Peter J. Albert and Ronald Hoffman (New York: Pantheon Books, 1990), 11–34; Lewis Baldwin, *There Is a Balm* (Philadelphia: Fortress Press, 1992), 189; and Preston N. Williams, "The Public and Private Burdens of Martin Luther King, Jr., *The Christian Century* (February 25, 1987): 198–99. Some of the works which examine convergences and differences in the two thinkers include: Lewis V. Baldwin, "Malcolm X and Martin Luther King, Jr.: A Reassessment of the Relationship Between Malcolm X and Martin Luther King, Jr." *Western Journal of Black Studies* 13, no. 2 (1989): 103–13; James H. Cone, *Martin and Malcolm and America: A Dream or a Nightmare* (Maryknoll, N.Y.: Orbis Books, 1991); Robert Michael Franklin, *Liberating Visions: Human Fulfillment and Social Justice in African-American Thought* (Minneapolis: Fortress Press, 1990); Robert Michael Franklin, *Harvard Divinity Bulletin* 21, no. 4 (1992). See also, Bruce Perry, *Malcolm: The Life of a Man Who Changed Black America* (Barrytown, N.Y.: Station Hill Press, 1991); Michael Dyson, "Who Speaks for Malcolm X! The Writings of Just About Everybody," *New York Times Book Review* (November 29, 1992), 33; Clayborne Carson, "Malcolm X: The Man and the Myth," *San Francisco Examiner*, November 22, 1992, D-9.

3 Cornel West, "Nihilism in Black America," *Race Matters* (Boston: Beacon Press, 1993), 8–20.

4 Moral leadership refers to "the process of morality to the degree that leaders engage with followers on the basis of shared motives

and values and goals." James MacGregor Burns, *Leadership* (New York: Harper and Row, 1979), 36. "The essence of leadership in any polity is the recognition of real need, the uncovering and exploiting of contradictions among values and between values and practice, the realigning of values, the reorganization of institutions where necessary, and the governance of change. Essentially the leader's task is consciousness-raising on a wide plane. . . . A congruence between the need and value hierarchies would produce a powerful potential for the exercise of purposeful leadership" (Burns, 43–44). In this sense, moral leadership is transformational as opposed to transactional (e.g., Weber's distinction between an ethic of responsibility versus an ethic of ends: the former seeks purposeful, cooperative change based on inclusiveness and equality; the latter maintains the status quo by minimizing conflict through hegemonic practices).

5 Daniel Defoe's *The Life and Adventures of Robinson Crusoe* is a classic, or as one commentator puts it, it is "universal and lasting." Written by Defoe and published in England in 1719, the book was translated into French, German, and Dutch the following year, marking an unprecedented series of translations into other languages. I make mention of its remarkable origins in order to underscore its availability and popular ascent in the European mindscape since the eighteenth century. In this respect, it is an exemplary text of the moral discourse and metaphysics of civilization. Ronald Takaki, *Iron Cages: Race and Culture in Nineteenth Century America* (New York: Oxford University Press, 1990), 108–44. "To speak means to be in a position to use a certain syntax, to grasp the morphology of this or that language, but it means above all to assume a culture, to support the weight of a civilization." Frantz Fanon, *Black Skin, White Masks* (London: Paladin, 1970), 13.

6 Charles E. Scott, *The Question of Ethics: Nietzsche, Foucault, and Heidegger* (Bloomington and Indianapolis: Indiana University Press, 1990).

7 Howard Thurman, *The Inward Journey* (Richmond, Ind.: Friends United Press, 1971, 1980), 38.

8 Howard Thurman, *With Head and Heart: The Autobiography of Howard Thurman* (San Francisco: Harcourt Brace Jovanovich 1979), 208.

9 Thurman, *Meditations of the Heart* (Richmond, Ind.: Friends United Press, 1976), 15.

10 Luther E. Smith, "Intimate Mystery: Howard Thurman's Search

for Ultimate Meaning (1900–1981)," in *Ultimate Reality and Meaning: Interdisciplinary Studies in the Philosophy of Understanding* 11 (June 1988):94–98. See also, John H. Cartwright, "The Religious Ethics of Howard Thurman," *Journal of the Interdenominational Theological Center* (Fall 1984/Spring 1985):22–34; and Walter G. Muelder, "The Structure of Howard Thurman's Religious Social Ethics," *Debate and Understanding*, ed. Ricardo A. Millet, Special Edition (Spring 1982):7–13; John Macmurray, *The Self As Agent* (London: Faber and Faber, 1957), 15; and Nicolas Berdyaev, *Slavery and Freedom* (New York: Charles Scribner's Sons, 1944), 47.

11 Howard Thurman, *The Creative Encounter* (Richmond, Ind.: Friends United Press, 1972) 46,49. See also his "Mysticism and Social Change: Mysticism—An Interpretation," *Eden Seminary Bulletin* (1939):3–10. Thurman, *Deep Is the Hunger* (Richmond, Ind.: Friends United Press, 1975), 62,64,93; and Thurman, "What Can I Believe In.?" *Journal of Religion and Healthy* 12 (November 1972):111–19; Thurman, Disciplines (Richmond, Ind.: Friends United Press, 1973), 57; and *Search for Common Ground* (New York: Harper and Row, 1971), 21.

12 Thurman, "The Inner Life and World Mindedness," in *Christian Leadership in a World Society: Essays In Honor of Conrad Henry Mochlman* (Rochester, N.Y.: Colgate Rochester Divinity School, 1945), 188.

13 Ibid.

14 Religious experience is defined by Thurman as "the conscious and direct exposure of the individual to God. Such an experience seems to the individual to be inclusive of all the meaning of his life—there is nothing that is not involved." Thurman, *Creative Encounter*, 20.

15 Thurman, *Creative Encounter*, 57. Rational coherence between the inner experience of self and the social world is the method employed to test for self-deception. He argues that "Whatever seems to deny a fundamental structure of orderliness upon which rationality seems to depend cannot be countenanced." Ibid, 57–58. Walter G. Muelder suggests that the underlying ethical theory which is operative in this construal is neither heteronomous, nor autonomous, but theonomous: "This means that the imperatives are not imposed from external sources, nor completely devised by inner personal mandates, but express at the deepest level a metaphysical divine moral order which is also the rational law of a person's own being. There is a meeting place for the communication between

God and the person, a place of yielding private, personal will to transcending purposes that are at the same time common ground. Here revelation and intuition meet, a place rich with the sense of the ultimate worth of the individual as a private and social person." Walter G. Muelder, "The Structure of Howard Thurman's Religious Social Ethics," 9; Nicolas Berdyaev argues that emergence from subjectivity proceeds along two distinct lines: objectivization and transcension or transcendence, the former leading to bondage because it alienates the divine image from itself which is personality, and the latter leading to authentic freedom because it raises the person to the level of the transubjective, to the realm of Spirit, which is freedom. See Berdyaev, *Slavery and Freedom*, 29.

16 Thurman, "He Looked For a City." Taped Sermon, Marsh Chapel, Boston University, January 2, 1955, Special Collections, Mugar Library, Boston University.

17 Ibid.

18 See Thurman, *Disciplines*, 26–37, where he discusses three primary questions related to the discipline of commitment. They are respectively, "Who am I?," "What do I want?," and "How do I propose to get it?"

19 Thurman, "He Looked For a City."

20 Thurman, *The Growing Edge* (Richmond, Ind.: Friends United Press, 1974), 68. See also, Thurman, *The Creative Encounter*, 115. Luther Smith's perceptive analysis of relationality as the hermeneutical key to Thurman is helpful. He cautions that "Thurman's introspective approach to reality and meaning should not be interpreted as a self-centered exercise. He begins with himself, but moves out to society as an arena of discovery and involvement. Thurman says that the sense of self may precede the sense of community and the history which forms it, but in fact the self is shaped by community. Community, and its history, precede the self; we are born into community." Smith, "Intimate Mystery," p. 91.

21 See Thurman, "Meaning is Inherent in Life," in *The Inward Journey*, 14–15.

22 Thurman explores these issues full-blown in *Jesus and the Disinherited* (Richmond, Ind.: Friends United Press, 1981); see also, Howard Thurman, *Temptations of Jesus: Five Sermons Given by Dean Howard Thurman in Marsh Chapel, Boston University*, 1962 (reprinted Richmond, Ind.: Friends United Press, 1978); and How-

ard Thurman, "The Hasty Word" in *The Creative Encounter*, 104–5.

23 Thurman, *The Temptations of Jesus*, 58–62.

24 This was the basis for Thurman's perception of the church as a resource for activists: "To me it was important that individuals who were in the thick of social change would be able to find renewal and fresh courage in the spiritual resources of the church. There must be provided a place, a moment, when a person could declare, 'I choose!'" Thurman, *With Head and Heart*, 160.

CAROLYN ANN KNIGHT: *Linking Texts with Contexts*

1 Ronald J. Sider and Michael King, *Preaching about Life in a Threatening World* (Philadelphia: Westminster Press, 1987), 12.

2 Christine M. Smith, *Preaching as Weeping, Confession, and Resistance: Radical Responses to Radical Evil* (Louisville: Westminster/John Knox Press, 1992), 1.

3 Ibid., 2.

4 Thomas H. Troeger, "The Social Power of Myth as a Key to Preaching on Social Issues," in *Preaching as a Social Act: Theology and Practice*, ed. Arthur Van Seters (Nashville: Abingdon Press, 1988), 211.

5 Ibid., 212.

6 Samuel D. Proctor, *Preaching about Crisis in the Community* (Philadelphia: Westminster Press, 1988), 11.

7 Sider and King, *Preaching about Life in a Threatening World*, 14.

8 Walter Brueggeman, "The Social Nature of the Biblical Text for Preaching," in *Preaching as a Social Act*, ed. Arthur Van Seters (Nashville: Abingdon Press, 1988), 127.

9 Ibid., 128.

10 Ibid.

11 Smith, *Preaching as Weeping, Confession, and Resistance*, 1.

12 Brueggeman, "The Social Nature of the Biblical Text," 129.

13 Troeger, "The Social Power of Myth as a Key to Preaching on Social Issues," 211.

14 J. Alfred Smith, "Preaching and Social Concerns," in *Handbook of*

Contemporary Preaching, ed. Michael Duduit (Nashville: Broadman Press, 1992), 512.

15 Troeger, "The Social Power of Myth as a Key to Preaching on Social Issues," 206, 208.

16 Henry H. Mitchell, *Black Preaching: The Recovery of a Powerful Art* (Nashville: Abingdon Press, 1990), 23.

17 Ibid., 20.

18 Ibid., 57.

19 Ibid., 56.

MARK V. C. TAYLOR: *What Can We Say to These Things?*

1 E. R. Carter, *Our Pulpit* (Chicago: Afro-Am Press, 1888, 1969), iv–v.

2 Regarding the response of white supremacists to the Civil Rights and Black Power Movements see Robert Allen, *Black Awakening in Capitalist America: An Analytic History* (Garden City, N.Y.: Anchor Books, 1970) and Harold Cruse, *Plural But Equal: A Critical Study of Blacks and Minorities and America's Plural Society* (New York: William Morrow, 1987), 269–391. The "suicidal impulse . . . " quote is taken from a conversation between Washington and the author during January 1995. Three important texts which analyze the continuing importance of mutating white supremacy are William Julius Wilson, *When Work Disappears: The New World of the Urban Poor* (New York: Vintage Books, 1996): Ellis Cashmere, *The Black Culture Industry* (London and New York: Routledge Books, 1997), and Haki Madhubuti, *Claiming Earth: Race, Rage, Rape, Redemption, Blacks Seeking a Culture of Enlightened Empowerment* (Chicago: Third World Press, 1994).

3 Frantz Fanon, *Black Skins, White Masks* (New York: Grove Press, 1967). George M. Fredrickson, *The Black in the White Mind: The Debate on Afro-American Character and Destiny, 1817–1914* (New York: Harper Torchbooks, 1971). Joel Kovel, *White Racism: A Psychohistory* (New York: Pantheon Books, 1970). Cornel West, *Prophesy Deliverance! An African-American Revolutionary Christianity* (Philadelphia: Philadelphia Press, 1982).

4 African American intelligence was attacked by Richard J. Herrnstein and Charles Murray's *The Bell Curve: Intelligence and Class Structure in American Life* (New York: Free Press, 1994). African American responsibility was attacked in Charles Murray's *Los-*

ing Ground: American Social Policy 1950–1980 (New York: Basic Books, 1984). African American beauty is attacked particularly in the popular media of TV and the movies. Recent movies have often bestialize Black men by likening them to space aliens, as in *Predator* and *Predator II* or the barroom monsters in *Gremlins* or the basketball playing monsters of *Space Jam.*

5 "Sermonic idea" was one of the terms used in a homiletics class at Union Theological Seminary, which I took in 1982. It was taught by Dr. James Forbes, who is currently Senior Pastor of the Riverside Church.

6 All references used here are taken from the Revised Standard Version.

GARY V. SIMPSON: *Preaching by Punctuation*

1 I am borrowing this phrase from his book by that same title. See Jacques Ellul, *The Humiliation of the Word* (Grand Rapids, Mich.: Eerdmans, 1985).

2 Frank Thomas, *They Like to Never Quit Praisin' God* (Cleveland: United Church Press, 1997), 3.

3 Clark Williamson and Ronald Allen, *The Teaching Minister* (Louisville: John Knox Press, 1991), 105.

4 Mihaly Csikszentmihaly, *Creativity* (New York: HarperCollins, 1996), 79.

5 Ibid.

6 See Henry Mitchell, *Celebration and Experience in Black Preaching* (Nashville: Abingdon Press, 1990).

DALE T. IRVIN: *Strangers and the Homecoming*

1 For a fuller discussion of the meaning of the term in the Mediterranean world and in the Bible, see John H. Elliott, *A Home for the Homeless: A Sociological Exegesis of I Peter, Its Situation and Strategy* (Philadelphia: Fortress Press, 1981), 27–49. The extent to which the early church understood itself through this term can be seen in the fact that the Greek word *paroikos* is the etymological root for the English word "parish."

2 "Epistle to Diognetus," Chapter 5 (translation my own).

3 The phrase comes from the title of the well-known work of Peter

Berger, Brigitte Berger, and Hansfried Kellner, *The Homeless Mind: Modernization and Consciousness* (New York: Random House, 1973).

4 I've borrowed the phrase from the title of James Melvin Washington's major historical study of the Black Baptist movement in the nineteenth century, *Frustrated Fellowship: The Black Baptist Quest for Social Power* (Macon, Ga.: Mercer University Press, 1986). In that book, Dr. Washington explored the unresolved dialectic between what can be broadly considered as the separatist and the integrationist impulses within the Black Baptist movement in the United States.

5 Matthew 8:20 and John 14:2.

6 Homi K. Bhabha, *The Location of Culture* (London and New York: Routledge, 1994), 9-10.

7 Washington, *Frustrated Fellowship*, 201-5.

8 Here, I am reading Marx as a philosopher and social theorist, not an economist.

9 Karl Marx, *Grundrisse: Foundations of the Critique of Political Economy*, trans. Martin Nicolaus (New York: Random House, 1973), 881.

10 Marx, *Grundrisse*, 882.

11 Johann Baptist Metz, *Faith in History and Society: Toward a Practical Fundamental Theology*, trans. David Smith (New York: Seabury Press, 1980), 88-99.

12 Irenaeus, "Against Heresies" (5.2.2), quoted from *The Ante-Nicene Fathers*, ed. Alexander Roberts and James Donaldson (Grand Rapids: Eerdmans, 1981), 1: 528.

LUCAS WILSON: *Seeming Silence and African-American Culture*

1 From James Melvin Washington *Conversations with God: Two Centuries of Prayers by African-Americans* (New York: HarperCollins, 1994), 284. This passage is from a prayer of benediction he wrote and dedicated to his dear friend and colleague, Cornel West.

2 Ibid., xxxvi.

3 James Melvin Washington, "Craven Images: The Eiconics of Race in the Crisis of American Church Historiography," in *The Agitated*

Mind of God: The Theology of Kosuke Koyama, ed. Dale T. Irvin and Akintunde E. Akinade (New York: Orbis Books, 1996), 139–40. Foucault's work on discourse theory is summarized in a useful volume, Sara Mills, *Discourse* (New York: Routledge, 1997).

4 See James Melvin Washington, *Frustrated Fellowship: The Black Baptist Quest for Social Power* (Macon, Ga.: Mercer University Press, 1986) and "Jesse Jackson and the Symbolic Politics of Black Christendom," in *Annals of the American Academy of Political and Social Science* 480 (July 1985): 89–105.

5 On the role of metaphor in Christian tradition, see Janet Martin Soskice, *Metaphor and Religious Language* (New York: Oxford University Press, 1985); Stuart Hall, "For Allon White: Metaphors of Transformation," in *Stuart Hall: Critical Dialogues in Cultural Studies*, ed. David Morley and Kuan-Hsing Chen (New York: Routledge, 1996), 287–88.

6 Hall, 287, emphasis added.

7 Washington, *Frustrated Fellowship*, 8.

8 Ibid., 7–22. See also Albert J. Raboteau, *Slave Religion* (New York: Oxford University Press, 1978), 152ff.

9 Theophus Smith "The Spirituality of Afro-American Traditions," in *Christian Spirituality: Post-Reformation and Modern*, ed. Louis Dupr and Don Saliers (New York: Crossroad Press, 1989), 373.

10 Stephen Crites, "The Narrative Quality of Experience," *Journal of the American Academy of Religion* 39 (1971): 295.

11 Ibid., 296.

12 Ibid.

13 See the inaugural lecture by James Melvin Washington, "The Grace of Interruptions: Towards a New Vision of Christian History," *Union Seminary Quarterly Review* 42, no. 4 (1988): 38.

14 See Washington, "Craven Images," 140–44.

15 Barbara Brown Taylor, *When God Is Silent* (Boston: Cowley Publications, 1998), 80. On West's description, see his dedication in *Restoring Hope: Conversations on the Future of Black America*, ed. Cornel West and Kelvin Shawn Sealey (Boston: Beacon Press, 1997).

16 This condensed passage is from a dialogue between James Washington, James Forbes, and Cornel West. The three began as col-

leagues on the faculty of Union Theological Seminary, where I first met them in 1983. In the years after, only Washington remained at Union. However, he cherished the fact that the three of them got together regularly for conversations much like this one. On this particular occasion, which took place December 18, 1996, at the Riverside Church in New York, their talk was part of a series of Town Meetings sponsored by the Obsidian Society and published as *Restoring Hope: Conversations on the Future of Black America*, 105, 111 (see n. 15).

CHERYL TOWNSEND GILKES: *"Some Folks Get Happy and Some Folks Don't"*

1   I Corinthians 12:4–5 (King James Version). This verse was used as the theme for *Women United*, the sixteenth-anniversary yearbook of the National Council of Negro Women organized by Mary McLeod Bethune.

2   The songs are seventeenth- and eighteenth-century hymns by Isaac Watts, Charles Wesley, and others that entered the African American oral tradition. Not only are they sung in a distinctive call-response style with the song leader "lining out" the words, but verses of these hymns have been absorbed into gospel music.

3   Michael W. Harris, *The Rise of Gospel Blues: The Music of Thomas Andrew Dorsey in the Urban Church* (New York: Oxford University Press, 1992).

4   The term "Sanctified Church" is indigenous to black communities and refers collectively to black holiness and pentecostal denominations and congregations. The term accounts for both the difference and kinship that simultaneously define the relationship between the Sanctified Church and the rest of the Black Church.

5   Joseph M. Murphy, *Working the Spirit: Ceremonies of the African Diaspora* (Boston: Beacon Press, 1994). Regarding "S/spirit(s)," Jualynne Dodson and I have chosen this construction as a way of talking across traditions that include both Christianity and African-derived religions and the shared features stemming from their emphasis on the Spirit or on orishas. See Jualynne E. Dodson and Cheryl Townsend Gilkes, " 'There's Nothing Like Church Food': Food and the U.S. Afro-Christian Tradition: Re-Membering Community and Feeding the Embodied S/spirit(s)." *Journal of the American Academy of Religion* 63 (1995), 519–38.

6   Matthew 18:20 (King James Version). The folk version of this is

sometimes stated, "Jesus said where two or three touch and agree, there will I be" and conflates verses 19 and 20 of that passage.

7 However, since so much attention is given to the role of the preacher, the roles of everyone else in "producing the sacred" tend to be ignored. Increasingly the preacher is cast as one of two extremes, villain or hero.

8 An extended discussion of Strauss's concept of the "negotiated order" and its implications and applications in social life can be found in John P. Hewitt's *Self and Society: A Symbolic Interactionist Social Psychology* (Boston: Allyn and Bacon, 1976).

9 Sidney W. Mintz and Richard Price, *The Birth of African American Culture: An Anthropological Perspective* (1976; Boston: Beacon Press, 1992).

10 Mintz and Price, 45.

11 Ibid, 45–46.

12 Murphy, *Working the Spirit.*

13 Dodson and Gilkes, "Church Food."

14 Miriam Therese Winter, Adair Lummis, and Allison Stokes, *Defecting in Place: Women Claiming Responsibility for their Own Spiritual Lives* (New York: Crossroad, 1994). See also Adair Lummis and Allison Stokes, "Catholic Feminist Spirituality and Social Justice Actions," *Research in the Social Scientific Study of Religion* 6 (1994): 103–38.

15 John Mbiti, *African Religions and Philosophy* (Garden City, N.Y.: Doubleday Anchor Books, 1969).

16 For a discussion distinguishing the syncretic from the symbiotic, see Leslie G. Desmangles, *The Faces of the Gods: Voudou and Roman Catholicism in Haiti* (Chapel Hill: University of North Carolina Press, 1992).

17 Zora Neale Hurston, *Moses, Man of the Mountain* (New York: J. B. Lippincott, 1939).

18 "He's a Battle Axe, in the time of trouble . . . ; shelter in the time of storm."

19 The image of the axe is also associated with the Yoruba orisha Shango.

20 John 4:24 (King James Version). Interestingly, Jesus makes this statement during his debate with the Samaritan women in which

they argue about the proper "place" for worship. Not only does Jesus assert the primacy of the Spirit in this exchange, but he also liberates worshippers from the authority of place, in this case, Jerusalem. Both issues would have been salient for Africans constructing an independent Protestant Christianity in the United States and providing grounding in contests between both Catholicism and Islam over the authority of place.

21 In a personal conversation, Mercy Amba Oduyoye described the complex religious consciousness of African women as stemming from their crucial role in maintaining their own traditions and teaching their husband's traditions to their children.

22 Margaret Washington Creel, *A Peculiar People: Slave Religion and Community Culture among the Gullahs* (New York: New York University Press, 1988). Also see Louise Meriweather's *Fragments of the Ark* (New York: Pocket Books, 1994), a novel set in the Sea Islands during the Civil War that provides vivid portrayals of black antebellum secret societies. See also Betty M. Kuyk, "The African Derivation of Black Fraternal Orders in the United States," *Comparative Studies in Society and History* 25 (October 1983): 559–92 as cited in Tera W. Hunter, *To 'Joy My Freedom: Southern Black Women's Lives and Labors after the Civil War* (Cambridge: Harvard University Press, 1997).

23 Arthur Huff Fauset, in his book *Black Gods of the Metropolis* (Philadelphia: University of Pennsylvania Press, 1944), discusses the Sanctified Church that he studied (Mt. Sinai Holy Church founded by Bishop Ida Robinson) as a sort of "graduate church" where people joined who were seeking a deeper, more intense religious experience.

24 W. E. B. Du Bois, "The Gift of the Spirit," in *The Gift of Black Folk: The Negro in the Making of America* (1924; New York: Washington Square Press, 1972).

25 W. E. B. Du Bois, "Of the Faith of the Fathers," in *the Souls of Black Folk* (1903; New York: Bantam Doubleday Dell, 1989), 139.

26 Du Bois, *The Gift of Black Folk.*

27 William L. Anderson, *Sisters of the Spirit: Three Black Women's Autobiographies of the Nineteenth Century* (Bloomington: Indiana University Press, 1986), 98–99.

28 Much of Du Bois's sociology focused on what is now called "agency"—the manner in which black people themselves responded to and challenged the constraining walls of social loca-

tion. Nathan Hatch has pointed to black religion as one of several major forces democratizing religion in America; see his *The Democratization of American Christianity* (New Haven: Yale University Press, 1989). On the other hand, Du Bois, in his very underappreciated little book *The Gift of Black Folk*, focused on the ways "black folk" with all of their gifts "reconstructed" and expanded democracy to make it more inclusive.

29 Du Bois, *Souls.*

LEE HANCOCK: *Letter to James*

1 David Hurst Thomas, the curator of North American Archeology at the American Museum of Natural History, explains that "Among the so called *Golden Isles*, St. Catherines Island is one of the few that have not been subdivided and suburbanized. The Georgia-based, not-for-profit St. Catherines Island Foundation owns the island and strictly regulates a comprehensive program of research and conservation. This enlightened and progressive land management policy insured that mission Santa Catalina not be destroyed by the crush of condos and fast food joints which typify too many of the southern barrier islands." David Hurst Thomas, *St. Catherines: An Island in Time* (Atlanta: Georgia Humanities Council, 1988), 1.

2 Ibid., 12.

3 The mission system that existed in Florida and Georgia rivaled the better known mission system established in the Southwest. Although contested, in fact the mission presence in the Southeast outstripped that of the Southwest in sheer numbers of friars present and missions established. As Thomas points out, "The numbers tell the story. The southeastern mission system was founded earlier, involved more people, and lasted longer than the southwestern system which is so familiar to Americans." Ibid., 3.

4 Thomas and others point out that the strength of the Spanish in the Southeast is a historical fact often overlooked by U.S. history told from the standpoint of the colonies in the Northeast. Thomas claims that America suffers from cultural amnesia regarding the role of the Spanish in the Southeast in general and in Georgia in particular. Ibid., 4–5.

5 I am gratefully indebted to my hosts, Dr. David Hurst, Thomas, Lorann S. A. Pendelton of the American Museum of Natural History, and Royce Hayes, Superintendent of St. Catherines Island,

for information in this essay furnished through extensive personal conversations.

6   Marion A. Habig, *The Alamo Chain of Missions: A History of San Antonio's Five Oldest Missions*, rev. ed., (Chicago: Franciscan Herald Press, 1976), 18.

7   Maynard J. Geiger, *The Franciscan Conquest of Florida (1573–1618)*, (Washington, D.C.: Catholic University of America, 1937), 88–89.

8   Thomas, *St. Catherines*, 13.

9   For further discussion of the concept of the gaze, see Michel Foucault, *Discipline and Punish: The birth of the Clinic* (New York: Vintage Books, 1975, 1995), chap. 3, part 3.

10 See Emile Durkheim, *The Elementary Forms of the Religious Life* (1915; New York: Free Press, 1965), 462 ff.

11 David Hurst Thomas et al., *The Anthropology of St. Catherines Island: Natural and Cultural History*, vol. 55, pt. 2 of the *Anthropological Papers of the American Museum of Natural History* (New York; American Museum of Natural History, 1978), 220–23.

12 James Melvin Washington, *Conversations with God: Two Centuries of Prayers by African Americans*, (New York: HarperCollins, 1994), xxxvi. At several points in this essay, I refer to ideas or expressions present in the brilliant introduction to this book. These "talking points" are not cited, but the direct quotations from this essay are.

13 Ibid., xxix.

14 John O'Donohue, *Anam Cara: A Book of Celtic Wisdom* (New York: HarperCollins, 1997), xvii.

15 See Martin Buber, *I and Thou* (New York: Charles Scribner's Sons, 1970), for a full discussion of this concept.

16 Dr. Dorothy Austin offered this insight in lecture in the spring of 1995 at the Graduate School, Drew University, Madison, N.J.

17 Washington, *Conversations with God*, xiv.

18 Ibid., xli. Washington utilizes Erik Erickson's concept of "pseudospeciation."

CONTRIBUTORS' NOTES

JAMES H. CONE is the Charles A. Briggs Distinguished Professor of Systematic Theology at Union Theological Seminary. He is the author of *Black Theology and Black Power*, as well as *Martin and Malcolm and America: A Dream or a Nightmare?*

DAVID D. DANIELS III is associate professor of Church History at McCormick Theological Seminary. An ordained minister of the Church of God in Christ, his research interests include the history of the holiness and Pentecostal movements in America.

QUINTON HOSFORD DIXIE teaches at Indiana University in the Department of Religious Studies.

WALTER E. FLUKER is professor of philosophy and religion and Executive Director of the Leadership Center at Morehouse College. He is also the president and founder of VisionQuest Association, Inc., which provides consulting and training in ethical leadership, and the editor and director of the Howard Thurman Papers Project.

CHERYL TOWNSEND GILKES is the John D. and Catherine T. MacArthur Associate Professor of Sociology and African-American Studies at Colby College and an Assistant Pastor at the Union Baptist Church in Cambridge, Massachussets. Her research areas include African American women and social change, as well as sociology of religion and African American religious history.

E. LEE HANCOCK was the first Seminary Pastor of Union Theological Seminary. She is completing her Ph.D. in Religion and Society at Drew University where she is an Adjunct Faculty member in the Theological School and program officer for the Newark Project.

VINCENT HARDING teaches at Iliff Theological Seminary in Denver, Colorado.

DALE T. IRVIN is professor of World Christianity at New York Theological Seminary and the author of *Christian Histories, Christian Traditioning: Rendering Accounts.*

CAROLYN ANN KNIGHT is the assistant professor of Preaching at the Interdenominational Theological Center in Atlanta, Georgia. She is the project director of the Gardner C. Taylor Preaching Archives and Listening Room at ITC. She is working on a book about the biblical sermon as social commentary.

CHARLES H. LONG retired from the University of California at Santa Barbara, where he was professor of History of Religions and director of the Research Center for Black Studies, in 1996. Prior to that time he was professor of History of Religions at the University of Chicago, professor of History of Religions at Duke University, the William Rand Kenan, Jr., Professor of History of Religions at the University of North Carolina at Chapel Hill, and the Jeannette K. Watson Professor of History of Religions at Syracuse University.

SANDY DWAYNE MARTIN is professor of Religion at the University of Georgia. Author of the book *Black Baptists and African Missions* and numerous articles on African American/American religious history, his most recently published book is *For God and Race: The Religious and Political Leadership of AMEZ Bishop James Walker Hood.*

GENNA RAE MCNEIL is professor of United States history and African American history at the University of North Carolina at Chapel Hill. She is the author of *Groundwork: Charles*

Hamilton Houston and the Struggle for Civil Rights, and is currently writing a book on Joan Little.

RICHARD NEWMAN is research officer at the W. E. B. Du Bois Institute for Afro-American Research at Harvard University. His most recent books include *Go Down Moses: Celebrating the African American Spiritual*, and *African American Quotations*.

ALBERT J. RABOTEAU is Henry W. Putnam Professor of Religion at Princeton University. The author *of Slave Religion: The "Invisible Institution" in the Antebellum South, A Fire in the Bones: Reflections on African-American Religious History*, and *African-American Religion*, Raboteau is also the co-editor of *African-American Religion: An Historical Interpretation with Representative Documents.*

GARY V. SIMPSON is senior pastor of the Concord Baptist Church of Christ in Brooklyn, New York. He has taught Preaching, Worship and Practical Theology at Drew, New Brunswick, New York, and Union Theological Seminaries.

MARK V. C. TAYLOR holds a Ph.D. in Church History from Union Theological Seminary. He is also the pastor of the Church of the Open Door in Brooklyn, New York.

JUDITH WEISENFELD is assistant professor of Religion at Barnard College. She is the author of *African-American Women and Christian Activism: New York's Black YWCA, 1905–1945*, and co-editor of *This Far by Faith: Readings in African American Women's Religious Biography*, and *The North Star: A Journal of African-American Religious History.*

CORNEL WEST is Alphonse Fletcher, Jr., University Professor at Harvard University. He is author of many books, including the best-selling *Race Matters, The American Evasion of Philosophy, The War Against Parents*, with Sylvia Ann Hewlett, and, most recently, *The Future of American Progressivism* with Roberto Unger.

LUCAS WILSON teaches economics and African American studies at Mount Holyoke College. His research is in Marxism, the history and methodology of economics, and African American Studies.

INDEX

Abraham, sacrifice of Isaac by, 169

activists, church as resource for, 245n24

Africa, worship traditions of, 34, 42

African American Christian spirituality: basis of, 203–4; in crisis, 211–13; as cultural force, 209–11; discourse of love in, 135; diversity and, 200–13; transcendence of, 213

African Americans: contemporary evangelicism of, 140; oral tradition, 250n2; religious liturgy of, 177; secularization in life of, 54; unity of, 106

Ahlstrom, Sidney, 196, 226

Alexander, Lucretia, 26

Allen, Richard, 46

Allen, Ronald, 149

American Africanism, 90

American Christendom, as opposition, xii

American Colonization Society, 46

American Passion Play, 160

Appiah, Anthony, 238n2

Arendt, Hannah, 177

"Aristocracy of Faith, The" (Washington), xiv

Armstrong, Karen, 4

Ashanti, 42

Atkinson, Henry, 26

Atlantic world, 16–18; and meaning of humanity, 15–16; origin of religion in, 11–21; passage to, 13–14; slave labor in, 18

Austin, J. C., 150

Baldwin, James, 78, 96, 101

Baptist history, black, xiii, 47. *See also* Washington, James

Barquaqua, Mohammed Gardo, 43

Barth, Karl, 123, 163, 225

Beckett, Samuel, 227

ben Said, Mohammed Ali, 43

Ben Solomon, Job, 43

Berdyaev, Nicolas, 244n15

Bernard of Clairvaux, 150

Bhabha, Homi K., 177

Bibb, Henry, 27

biblical exegesis, 158

Bilali, Salih, 43

Black Christian Consensus, 40–60, 53–54; challenge to, 54–56; formation of, 41–44; revitalization of, 56–60

black church: diversity of, 202–5; emergence of, 47

Black Laws, 64

black nationalists, 81

Black Panther party, 134

Black Power movement, 79, 82–83; love in, 134

black religion: as democratizer, 252–53n28; and integration, 80–81; justice, love, and hope in, 74–85; politics of, 185

Black Theology, 59–60, 135; development of, 83–85

Blassingame, John, 50

Bonhoeffer, Dietrich, 68

Bowen, John Wesley Edward, xiii

Braudel, Fernand, 14–15

Brueggeman, Walter, 127–28

Bryan, Andrew, 27